Superb eLearning Using Low-cost Scenarios: A Step-by-Step Guide to *eLearning by Doing*

This book explains step-by-step how to create really superb e-learning that incorporates scenarios in a simple easy-to-follow way. It contains:

20 How to Techniques

28 Best Practices

36 Guidelines

9 Key Points

28 Tips

16 Warnings

25 Critical Success Factors

115 Examples

But Is This Guide for You?

Warning 1: This guide it is not for everyone. It is only for the serious designers.

This guide is for e-learning instructional designers who:

- ✓ Want to increase the *effectiveness* of their courses. If you just want to do something more *interesting*, then you have the wrong book. If you just want to join the latest trend, then you have the wrong book. This is for people who are serious about e-learning and its impact.

- ✓ Have a foundation in e-learning instructional design (defining the course purpose and target audience, data gathering, writing objectives, solid instructional design principles, best practices in course layout, etc.) If you don't, you should get the companion book, *Designing Effective eLearning* (2013), and then go and write a couple of courses.

- ✓ Have designed several linear e-learning courses and are aware of the limitations of the authoring tool to be used to convert their design into a computer-based training course.

About the Author

Ben Pitman is a training and instructional design professional with over 20 years of experience. He is a Certified Internet Webmaster and holds a Ph.D. in Human Resource Development. He has been developing e-learning courses for over 10 years. He has helped thousands of people with Lectora problems on the community forum and is known there as "Dr. Lectora."

Ben is available for consulting on e-learning design or development in Lectora. Here is his contact information:

- Ben.pitman@eProficiency.com
- 678-571-4179 in Atlanta, GA
- See www.eProficiency.com to learn more

Other Books by Benjamin Pitman

Effective eLearning Design series:

Vol. 1: Designing Effective eLearning: A Step-by-Step Guide

Vol. 2: Superb eLearning using Low-Cost Scenarios: A Step-by-Step Guide to eLearning by Doing

Vol. 3: ILT to CBT (due 2015)

Mastering Lectora® series:

Lectora 101: Ten Easy Steps for Beginners

Lectora 201: What They Don't Tell You in Class

Lectora 301: Techniques for Professionals (due 2014)

Business Process Reengineering: Plain and Simple (1990)

Superb eLearning Using Low-cost Scenarios:

A Step-by-Step Guide to eLearning by Doing

Edition 1.0

Benjamin Pitman, Ph.D.

© Copyright 2014, Benjamin Pitman, Suwanee, GA, USA

eProficiency, Inc.
1810 Chattahoochee Run Drive
Suwanee, GA 30024
678-571-4179
www.eProficiency.com

No part of this publication may be reproduced, stored in a retrieval system, or transmitted in any form or by any means, electronic, mechanical, photocopying, recording, scanning, or otherwise, except as permitted under Section 107 or 108 of the 1976 United States Copyright Act, without the prior written permission of the Author. Requests to the Author for permission should be addressed to the Permissions Department, eProficiency, Inc. 1810 Chattahoochee Run Dr., Suwanee, GA 30024, 678-571-4179, email: support@eproficiency.com.

Limit of Liability/Disclaimer of Warranty: While the publisher and the author have used their best efforts in preparing this document, they make no representations or warranties with respect to accuracy or completeness of the contents of this document and specifically disclaim any implied warranties of merchantability or fitness for a particular purpose. The advice and strategies contained herein may not be suitable to your situation. You should consult with a professional where appropriate. Neither the publisher nor the author shall be liable for any loss of profit or any other commercial damages, including but not limited to special, incidental, consequential, or other damages.

For general information on other products and services including training and coaching, or technical support, please visit www.eProficiency.com or contact Ben Pitman at 678-571-4179, support@eProficiency.com.

Trademarks: Windows®, Microsoft®, Microsoft® Word, and PowerPoint® are registered trademarks of Microsoft Corporation. Lectora® is a registered trademark of Trivantis Corporation. Flash® is a registered trademark of Adobe Systems Inc. Other product and company names mentioned herein may be the trademarks of their respective owners. Use of trademarks or product names is not intended to convey endorsement or affiliation with this book.

Library of Congress Cataloging-in-Publication Data
Pitman, Benjamin.
    Superb eLearning Using Low-cost Scenarios: A Step-by-Step Guide to eLearning by Doing
Includes bibliographical references and index.

ISBN-13: 978-1495215179

ISBN-10: 1495215172

1. E-learning design. 2. Scenarios. 3. Training design. 4. Computer-based training design, 5. Web-based training design

To my nephew, Cliff Perry,
who helps me think outside the box.

And of course, to my wife who always shed
light on those dark days.

Contents

Introduction—1
What Is the Problem with Current Courses?—5
What It Is and What It Is Not—11
Why It Works—14
When to Use It—15
How to Sell This to Your Boss or Client—17
Coming Up Next—19

Task 1: Define the Basis for Your Course—23
What's Going on Here?—23
Step 1: Find Out Who Cares About This Training—24
Step 2: Find Out What the Course Sponsor is Trying to Accomplish—26
Step 3: Nail-down Who the Trainees Are—31
Step 4: Define Specifically What They Need To Be Able To Do—35
Step 5: Review with Key Stakeholders—44
Critical Success Factors—45

Task 2: Collect Your Content—47
Step 1: Collect Basic Content—48
Step 2: Collect Content for the Scenario—52
Step 3: Organize & Chunk Content—56
Step 4: Review and Revise Course Purpose and Objectives—57
Step 5: Review with Major Stakeholders—58
Critical Success Factors—58

Task 3: Create a Rough Draft—61
What's Going on Here?—61
Step 1: Briefly Outline How You Are Going to Deliver Your Content—64
Step 2: Draft a Great Scenario Opening—65
Step 3: Plan the Interactions—71
Step 4: Draft Scoring, Results, and Debriefing Approach—82
Step 5: Make Strategic Decisions Regarding Media—85
Step 6: Draft the Interface—85
Step 7: Review with Stakeholders—91

Critical Success Factors—92

Task 4: Build a Prototype—93
What's Going on Here?—94
Step 1: Create the Screen Layout—95
Step 2: Create Typical Pages—99
Step 3: Review with Stakeholders—102
Critical Success Factors—103

Task 5: Draft a Storyline If Needed—105
What's Going on Here?—105
Step 1: Envision a "Story-*world*", Not a Story—107
Step 2: Use the Tried and True Hollywood Formula—109
Step 3: Review/Refine the Scenario Situation and Goal—110
Step 4: Identify Obstacles/Problems for Interactions—111
Step 5: Write Character Descriptions—111
Step 6: Write the Story—112
Step 7: Remove the Boring Bits → Make It Fun—113
Step 8: Review with Stakeholders—114
Critical Success Factors—114

Task 6: Write the Final Storyboard—117
Why a Storyboard?—117
What's Going on Here?—118
A Word about Consistency—120
Step 1: Select Your Storyboarding Tool—121
Step 2: Write Your Course Opening Section—121
Step 3: Write Your Content Section—127
Step 4: Write Your Scenario Opening Pages—129
Step 5: Write the Scenario Interactions—132
Step 6: Finalize the Results, Results Section—155
Step 7: Write the Wrap-up Section—160
Step 8: Write the Support Section—160
Step 9: Finish Up—161
Critical Success Factors for "eLearning by Doing"—166

Appendix 1: "Forms" to Help with Design—169

Scenario Course Rough Draft Form—170
Storyline Form—171
Interaction Form—172

Appendix 2: Book Highlights—175

References—187

Index—189

Introduction

We learn best by doing and from our mistakes – i.e. learning by doing. The trick is how can we, as e-learning designers, implement learning by doing with a very small budget? If you want to know the answer, read on.

This is a companion book to my earlier book, *Designing Effective eLearning: A Step-by-Step Guide*. Small amounts of critical information from that book are reproduced here, but in most cases, it is abridged.

My focus for this guide is on you creating better courses, not on perfect grammar or beautiful graphics. Personally, I get bored with formal third-person documents that explain how to do things. I intentionally, I wrote it as if I were talking directly to you. Here and there, I took a few liberties with the English language (no fainting). Mainly, rather than put "he/she" or default to "he" or swap arbitrarily back and forth between "he" and "she," I used "they" in many cases. Once in a while you may find incomplete sentences like you would use when you are talking to someone. Just remember my intent – to help you to write better e-learning courses.

I write using a lot of bullets and tables. I am not one for long wordy explanations or summarizing research. The work here is mostly based on the research of others and I could not have written it without their work, especially Ruth Clark.

How This Guide Is Organized

The main purpose of this first chapter is to help you sell using scenarios to your boss or to a client. It grounds you in what scenario-based learning is and why you should consider using it. It explains why it works so well.

The following chapters walk you through the tasks and steps to build a course that uses scenarios when you have a limited budget.

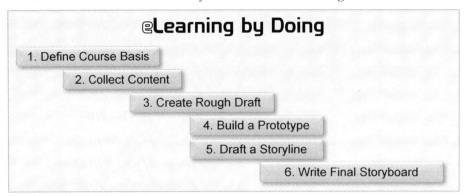

Symbols and Terms

Most of these are obvious, but just in case, here is your heads up. All but the last one are summarized in Appendix 2: Book Highlights.

Key Point: This symbol, a key, indicates particularly important stuff that is key to writing a scenario-based course. It is not something you do, but something you should know so you can make better decisions about your designing effective courses.

Technique: This tells you here is an effective way to do something. It usually has a few steps that are easy to follow.

Best Practice: This indicates a best practice. Try your best to follow these practices when developing your scenario course.

Guideline: This indicates an important tip to guide you along the way. Many times, you will have choices about doing something. These tips are important in helping you make the right decision.

Warning: This indicates an area you should exercise caution.

This symbol indicates an iterative process. It would be nice if we could just start at the beginning and go straight on to the end. However, life is not like that. In most areas, you will working on some step or task and realize you need to refine an earlier one. You don't have enough content, your performance objectives need to change, your prototype needs to be updated, etc., or as you well know, someone who said yesterday said it was fine, and today says you need to make major changes!

And just to be clear, here is how I use a few of the more common words that appear in e-learning literature.

Term	How I Used It
Course	Lesson or module – I make no distinction between these in this book.
Design	I use "design" to refer to the entire process of figuring out what you are going to present and how you will do it. This covers creating an outline through building a storyboard.
Development	I use "develop" to refer to the process of taking the storyboard and moving it into an authoring tool that will present the content online.
Job – as in "on the job"	The environment where the content is to be applied. Usually this the usual work environment but it really means anywhere learners will *use* the content.
Course Purpose	The *business* need tied to the training objective. "The purpose of this course is to increase productivity by improving managers' skill in coaching employees." Some might refer to this as the "terminal objective."

Term	How I Used It
Scenario Goal	The objective of the scenario (to sell xxx units, diagnose yyy, evaluate zzz …) (To minimize confusion in this book, I use "purpose" for *course* goal or the classic, "terminal objective." I reserve the word "goal" for the goal of the scenario.)
Scenario	A series of questions presented to the learners set in a *realistic* setting and *involving the learner as a participant*. A role-play exercise in an e-learning course. "A customer walks in and asks about the new cell phone. See if you can answer his questions about the new phone and make the sale." This plus the questions (decisions) that follow make up the scenario.
Simulation	A very life-like computer environment where the learner is an active participant like an airplane simulator or some kind of military battle. Simulations are generally more realistic and much more complex to develop than scenarios.
Stakeholders	Anyone who cares about this course and its effects. This includes your boss, his boss, sponsors, SMEs, target learners, potential buyers, and corporate vigilante departments like HR, Legal, and Communications. Know who they are and keep them in the loop so you don't run into roadblocks.

How to Get the Most Out of This Guide

Warning 2: Don't try to read this guide all at once.

Start out by giving it a quick once-over. Look over the table of contents and figure out how it is organized. Read Appendix 2: Book Highlights. Then grab your first course and dive in. As you begin each task, read that chapter in this guide. Go do it. Then come back and review the chapter to be sure you did not leave anything out.

What Is the Problem with Current Courses?

There is a problem with our regular courses – they are not terribly effective. Many of the current attempts make the course a bit more interesting but not more effective. Myths persist around why we can't do better but they are just myths. There is a solution, as we shall see.

The Problem - Ineffectiveness

Knowledge/information is not enough. In most cases, it is useless and gets in the way!

> *"Information by itself is meaningless. It only holds value if the learner knows what to do with it. You want to know how the learner will use the information and then build your scenarios around that."* Tom Kuhlmann (2008)

It is the *application* of information by learners that is what counts – using information to → increase skills → that leads to increased performance. But many times our training efforts do not work or at least not very well.

We are producing a lot of courses but many, dare I say most, are *not* producing the desired results. The learners don't remember what they were supposed to or worse, they don't use it. Why? Because the courses either:

- Are not engaging enough to hold their interest or
- Are not closely connected to their job to support transfer to the job or
- Do not provide enough practice for the learner to remember the content or remember to use the content.

Current Attempts to Solve the Ineffectiveness Problem Fail

Warning 3: Many e-learning designers and developers fruitlessly try to make their courses better by adding slick graphics, animations, audio, video, having a lot of things the learner to click on, and simple recall questions.

Let's see why these don't do the job as well as you might expect. Some don't cost much while others require a heavy investment and yield little improvement.

Inadequate Techniques to Make a Course Effective

Inadequate Technique	Impact on Learning	Cost/Effort to Produce
1. Click to see more info	*Negative* to very low Clicking on something to see more information is *not* interaction. It does *not* make the course more interesting. It does prove they are awake. It slows the learner down. The only real reason to use "click to see" is for *optional* material. Some people want more detail while others do not. Use it *only for optional* material.	Low. If you require the learner to click on everything, then what happens when they come back to the page? Effort to do this goes up more.
2. Animations	Low to moderate Animations help when you want to make a point or when trying to illustrate something that involves a sequence of events like a process or an engine working. Ruth Clark has found that in some cases *more* is retained when you use simple *still* pictures.	Moderate to high.

Inadequate Technique	Impact on Learning	Cost/Effort to Produce
3. Slick graphics	*Negative* to low The course is more pleasing to look at *but* these usually do not help the learner retain more. They do "sell" the course to promoters and potential customers, management, and yes, learners like them. However, in the end, they do *not* significantly increase learning. Linda Lohr (p 114) reminds us that *eliminating* unneeded detail makes learning more effective *by focusing the learners' attention on critical information*. Slick graphics frequently provide *more* rather than *less* detail and thus get in the way.	Low to moderate.
4. Simple recall questions	Low to moderate Simple recall questions like "Which of these helps reduce stress?" simply has the learner recall what was covered. Yes, that is repetition and that is good. However, when you consider what else you could do with almost the same amount of design time and time on the learners' part, it is poor. They do not involve the learner nor do they help transfer the skills to the job.	More than "click to see" but much less than some of the others.

Inadequate Technique	Impact on Learning	Cost/Effort to Produce
5. Over-the-counter games	Low Many if not most games you can buy to add to your course use a setting that is not job related thus minimizing transfer of the content to work. Many use True/False questions. Soon learners realize that they really don't need to answer the questions but rather just pick one of the choices. Even if you make a certain score required, the learner can still answer the questions without having to really apply the content.	Usually low to medium
6. Audio for ordinary content	Low Using audio to present ordinary material will result in learners retaining *less* and becoming frustrated at the rigid pace. Most people remember more when they see material rather than hear it. Yes, there are exceptions. Make both available.	Moderate. Audio is much harder to review and correct than text. Also, you now have to worry about sound levels and if the learner is in a place where they can listen without disturbing others.
7. Audio for special content	Moderate to high Ruth Clark has found through research that audio is *very* useful when explaining a graphic. The learner sees the graphic and hears the explanation. Other researchers have found that it is useful in teaching affective domain content like interpersonal skills.	

Inadequate Technique	Impact on Learning	Cost/Effort to Produce
8. Video	Low to high Video, like animations, is useful to make a point. It is also very useful when teaching affective domain content the same way audio is. But again, more is *not* better. However, they can be effectively used in scenarios as we shall see.	Moderate to high It has to be closely scripted and acted well. A talking head from the CEO to open a course is easy but one to show how to talk to an upset employee needs people who can act.

Excuses for Not Doing Better

So, people are doing all this, sometimes at great expense, and yet there is not much improvement. Okay, so what else could we do?

One answer would be to use scenarios or simulations. But we don't see very many of them out there. **Why?** The answers I have heard are:

- **Excuse: Not thinking of it** – Many are unfamiliar with the concept and so do not even think of using them.
- **Excuse: Lack of Time** – Simulations and scenarios take a lot longer to develop.
- **Excuse: Lack of Know-how** – Simulations and scenarios require additional skills most of us don't have yet.
- **Excuse: Lack of Resources** – Simulations and scenarios take a lot more effort to create.

Myths

Well, guess what? Three of these are myths for scenarios. Simulations need to be as realistic as possible and thus require very good graphics and technology as well as a great script/storyline. To do this requires time, know-how, and resources. But the same is *not* true of scenarios!

- **Know-how** – Scenarios do require some minimal additional skills but nowhere near as many or complex as most people believe. Most are covered in this book. It usually does *not* involve advanced technical skills or story writing skills. If they did, *I* would never do it and this book would not exist!

- **Time** – Of course, scenarios take a longer to develop because there are more pages and questions. But some developers think it takes 2-3 times as much time and effort. Not so. It is more like the amount of time it takes to add 5-20 well-thought-out questions to a course. This is very doable.

- **Resources** – Scenarios do take more effort but *not* a *lot* more effort to create. You usually can do it with your current staff and e-learning tools. Scenarios do *not* require 3D or animation, both of which take very specialized tools and people to use them effectively like simulations do.

The Solution

The answer is to shift from "simulation" thinking to something more like "situation-based", "problem-based" or "role-play" e-learning. This kind of course can be highly engaging.

> *"In other words, engagement makes people care about their performance; it makes them want to do their best."* **Kathleen Iverson's** article on Engaging the E-Learner: Interaction is Not Education. e-magazine, Feb 2008.

> *"'Guided discovery' learning methods, such as scenario-based e-Learning, have been proven to be more effective than pure 'discovery learning' because they provide guidance, structure and focused-goals."* (Ruth Clark, 2013)

> *"Learners are more motivated by scenario-based e-learning than by traditional instruction."* (Ruth Clark, 2013)

> *"Scenario-based e-learning accelerates expertise."* (Ruth Clark, 2013)

> *"... regardless of location, whether it be a simulator [a scenario,] or OJT, the participant needs to feel actually included instead of just merely an observer."* Cliff Perry, personal email, 2013.

> *"People do not learn as much until they are actually placed in the actual scenario, so in essence, they need to be actually placed within realistic representations of what those scenarios might be, rather than just a multiple choice or true/false question.* Cliff Perry, personal email, 2013.

By presenting the right type of situation in a scenario, you can get the learner to *think* and make decisions which helps them:

- understand the course content,
- remember it longer, and
- be more likely to actually use it when the need arises.

What It Is and What It Is Not

In some ways, you can think of scenarios as providing some content and then placing the learner in a role-play exercise.

> *"A traditional course would be like the computer manufacturer giving me a handbook with all of the information on how to repair a computer. A scenario-based course would be like a real situation where I actually need to make the choices that are part of repairing a computer. Both approaches give me the course content. But instead of just reviewing it, I'm presented with a problem and then use the information to solve it. I think you'd agree that actually solving the problem becomes a better learning experience than just seeing the information."* (Tom Kuhlmann, 2008)

> *"Scenario-based e-learning is a preplanned guided inductive learning environment designed to accelerate expertise in which the learner assumes the role of an actor responding to a work-realistic assignment or challenge, which in turn responds to reflect the learner's choices."* (Clark, 2013)

Essentially, scenarios are a role-play exercise from the classroom taken to e-learning. They are an e-learning approach in which a real situation is presented to enable the learner to practice key job skills, steps, or tasks.

Key Characteristics

The key characteristics of scenario-based e-learning – that is, learning by doing – are:

- Learners are presented with *realistic job-related situations.*
- *They* are placed *in* the situation (an actor in the story).
- They to make *realistic* decisions, predictions, calculations, or give explanations.
- They receive information about the potential *consequences* of their decisions not just "correct" or "incorrect."

Remember the above. These characteristics make all the difference in the world. **They make "learning by doing."**

Directive E-learning vs. Scenario-based

The scenario-based course design looks a little different from your standard linear or directive e-learning course.

Standard Course vs. One with a Scenario

Standard Directive	Scenario-Based
Read, listen to, watch content, with maybe a few exercises.	Some of this but then, think through a problem and make a decision.
Learning objectives	Performance based objectives
Focus is on content structuring, usually hierarchical built from simple to more complex.	Focus is on a realistic scenario design with content embedded in the course.
If there is a case study, the lesson usually ends with it as a way to wrap-up the lesson.	The lesson begins with the case description and serves as a vehicle to present content (Clark, 2013, p. 8).

Standard Directive	Scenario-Based
The learner's role is to absorb the content and respond to questions about the content.	The learner's role is an actor to make key decisions regarding action choices.
Usually there is a low to moderate level of interactivity.	Usually there is a high level of interactivity.
If there are exercises, they are usually *not* connected to each other.	In the scenario, the problems are related to a common situation or storyline.
The questions are about the content with distractors being other aspects of the content.	The questions ask for a decision adapted to the job environment rather than just the content.
Distractors are just distractors and not necessarily related to the job or experience.	Distractors are common misunderstandings, mistakes, and misconceptions.
The feedback is usually right/wrong with possible restatement of content.	The feedback is within context of the scenario and includes natural consequences of choice/decision (intrinsic feedback).
It may or may not put any emphasis on learning from mistakes.	There is heavy emphasis on learning from mistakes.
There is usually no scoring except for tests.	Frequently there is some type of scoring or rating of overall performance like sales or productivity.
Navigation is usually linear.	Navigation can be linear or can branching or may not be needed.

Standard Directive	Scenario-Based
Learner is focused on reviewing material.	Learner is focused on performing some sort of task, solving a problem, predicting outcomes, or explaining what just happened.
Content is usually presented in a linear fashion based on some structure.	Content can be delivered in a variety of ways, not necessarily in a linear fashion.

What It Is Not

Scenarios are not:

- ✗ A game (Because most games are *not* job related)
- ✗ A case study followed by questions (Although very useful, they usually do not involve the learner as a participant.)
- ✗ A simulation (Because most simulations are usually much more complex to script and build)

Why It Works

Engagement increases mastery. Here is what few of the experts in the field have to say.

> *"Many positive outcomes in performance are linked to engagement. Steven Brown and Thomas Leigh found that when individuals are personally engaged in an activity, they have more stamina; they will try harder when facing an obstacle, and perform better. L. Dee Fink found that engaged learners are also more likely to apply the learned concepts and transfer them to new situations. Thomas Britt found that engagement has implications for motivation and performance and the emotional consequences following the outcome of performance. Personal engagement in an activity magnifies the emotional consequences of succeeding versus failing at a task, because performance outcomes have greater implications for the individual's identity. In other words, engagement makes people care about their performance; it makes them*

want to do their best." Kathleen Iverson's article on Engaging the E-Learner: Interaction is Not Education. e-magazine, Feb 2008.

"Humans tend to ... readily forget information they have received outside contexts of actual use..." (Gee, 2003, p. 113)

"Human beings are quite poor at using verbal information when given lots of it out of context and before they can see how it applies to actual situations. They use verbal information best [emphasis added] when it is given "just in time" (when they can put it to use) and 'on demand' (when they feel they need it)." (Gee, 2007, p. 37)

Malcolm Knowles taught us that "adults learn best when they have a need to know."

In other words, learners are more likely to *remember* and *apply* what is learned if they have to *apply* content as part of the learning experience instead of just seeing it. Bottom line? *Scenarios create a need to know.* This is why we need to create scenarios that resemble the workplace that involve the learner as actors.

When to Use It

You can use it with just about any kind of adult training but it seems to be a little better suited to:

- Learners who already have a little relevant knowledge and
- Content that involves cognitive functions beyond simply recall.

Here are a few examples

- Coaching
- Supervisor training
- Sales training
- Interpersonal skills
- Ethics training
- Training to sell a new product
- Analysis, diagnosis

- Assessment, evaluation
- Project planning

Ruth Clark (2013) lists these situations that call for scenario-based e-learning:

Situations that Call For Scenarios

Situation	Examples
1. Rare occurrence tasks	- Trouble shooting - Handling employee outbursts - Handling discipline problems
2. Critical thinking skills training	- Trouble shooting - Strategic planning - Assessment, Evaluation - Diagnosis
3. Compliance-mandated training	- Information security - Safety - Ethical conduct
4. Lengthy timeline tasks	- Designing anything complex (like an e-learning course) - Developing a computer software system
5. High risk tasks	- Defusing a bomb - Combat tactics - Negotiation

To generalize, use scenarios with any kind of training that involves learning where there is a need to use policies, principles, procedures, or some kind of skill.

What about Stuff They Should Just Know?

This is my personal take on this. Unlike the rest of this book, I have no research to back this up.

If your course covers something that the learner will *not* use, why are you teaching it? It must be used somewhere! Start asking questions like:

- **When would they ever be actually using this? How?**
- **What would they be using it for?**
- **What would happen if they did not know this?**

Tip 1: If you don't get good answers to these questions, why are you wasting time on this?

My favorite example here is an orientation course where you cover when the company was founded and who key managers are.

- When would an employee *use* the date the company was founded? When a customer walks into the store and asks how long you have been in business.
- When would an employ *use* who the managers are? When something is going wrong and the appropriate manager needs to be notified.

Consider Using It for Tests

Instead of the boring and sometimes scary test, use a scenario. It helps learners transfer the knowledge to the workplace as well as finding out just how much they know. Do you like taking a test? I don't! Well, I don't think your learners will be much different. A scenario takes the pressure off a bit and makes it more fun and interesting while at the same time making it more likely they will apply the content.

How to Sell This to Your Boss or Client

At first bosses, clients, or stakeholders (managers, etc.) may resist using scenarios in their courses. To convince them, here are a few advantages.

Advantages over the Standard Push Approach

Scenario-based training courses usually increase mastery better than simple linear courses. Why are they better for the learner?

- **Scenarios tap into the adult preference for practical application.**
- **They create a "need to know"** grounded in the real-world rather than simply pushing information.
- **They allow the learner to learn from their mistakes** (experimentation, learning by doing) - one of the primary ways we learn which is usually not supported in page-turning approach.
- **The learner has a high level of engagement** in the learning experience.
- **They tie the information to the job** instead of just an abstract set of information thereby increasing transfer.

Why are they better for the business?

- **More is remembered** due to higher level of engagement.
- **More is actually used** on the job because the more realistic settings enable higher transfer to the workplace.
- **The business goals of the course are more likely to be achieved.**

Due to the engaging nature of scenarios, the brain has to connect more pieces. In the process, retention increases.

Due to the engaging nature, most people (not all) find scenario-based more interesting and so pay more attention and are more likely to finish.

Back to Convincing Your Boss or Client

You already have plenty of ammunition from the above. But in case you want some more ideas, try this.

Technique 1: How to convince your boss or client to use a scenario:

1. Start by asking your boss or client *why* they are doing training in the first place. Hopefully you will get an answer that is something like:
   - Increase the bottom line
   - Give our organization the advantage with high ROI on training dollars – skills not just courses
   - Increase performance/productivity
   - Achieve success
   - Avoid law suits
   - Reduce errors, problems, accidents, defects

2. Ask your boss: "While most training focuses on information, its real focus should be *not* on the information but on *using it* – building skills and being more productive (safer, less error prone, …). Isn't that what you want?" If you don't get a good answer to this, polish up your résumé, and start looking for someone who really cares about the outcome of the courses.

3. If you get an answer to the "why" question something like, "The ___ requires it" then come back with, "Why is that regulation in place?" The answer usually is to increase safety or reduce negative outcomes. Build from there.

Coming Up Next

Before we can lay out a plan, we need to know where we are going. Let's begin with a high-level view of a scenario-based e-learning course. This is certainly *not* cast in stone but most scenario courses have these sections somewhere.

High-level Scenario Course Structure

For the purposes of this book, I will discuss these components in the order shown but you could have a very different arrangement.

Sections of a Scenario Course

Section	Contents/Components		
1. Opening Pages	Welcome/splash, introduction, qualification questions, expectations (objectives), benefits, set the stage, etc.		
2. Content	Abbreviated content as some can and probably should be delivered within the scenario (learn by doing)		
3. Scenario	Opening	Scenario challenge, interface/ navigation instructions page(s), learner customization page(s) if any	
	Interaction Segments	Interactions where learners make decisions (usually questions but not always) and get feedback	
	Results	Summary of how they did with as much analysis as possible and debriefing	
4. Wrap-up	Summary of what was covered, key points to remember and next steps		
5. Support	Popup pages containing any kind of support material used by learners		

How We Will Get This Done

We tackle creating a course with these sections in six tasks, each broken down into steps.

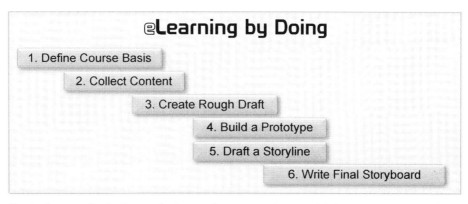

Each chapter includes techniques, best practices, guidelines, tips, examples, and warnings.

Overview of Scenario Course Design Tasks

Task	What's Included
1. Define the Basis for Your Course	First, we get clear about whom the stakeholders are and what they are trying to accomplish. Then, as usual, we get a picture of our target audience so we know whom we are writing for.
2. Collect Content	This is pretty much the usual fair of pulling together content **but with an emphasis on collecting "war stories" (mistakes and lessons learned)** from the SMEs or other experienced people.
3. Create a Rough Draft	This is a *rough* draft of the course, not the final storyboard because the next two tasks have a great deal of impact on your overall design. Also, you want to run your idea by the stakeholders before you invest a lot of time and effort into it only to find they have different ideas.
4. Build a Prototype	While this may seem a bit premature, it is a good idea because you may find limitations you had not expected. Also, you can get early approval from your stakeholders which frequently does not go as quickly as you thought it would.

Task	What's Included
5. Draft a Storyline	Some scenarios call for a storyline. If yours does, this is when you draft it.
6. Write the Final Storyboard	Finally, you take your rough draft, what you learned from building a prototype, and your storyline, and create your storyboard.

Tip 2: The tasks are presented linearly but in reality they overlap. From the beginning, you should know that you are likely *not* done with any task until the course is completely developed. In all likelihood, you will be going back for more information on typical problems faced, cues to solve the problems, more war stories, etc.

Task 1: Define the Basis for Your Course

What's Going on Here?

We do the standard bits about finding out who wants this course, who will get it, and what it is supposed to do.

The steps and deliverables in this task are:

24 Task 1: Define the Basis for Your Course

Step	Deliverables
1. Find out who cares about this training	List of stakeholders and what they expect from the course
2. Find out what the course sponsor is trying to accomplish	Course purpose
3. Nail-down who the trainees are	Target audience description
4. Define what they need to be able to do	Performance objectives
5. Review with stakeholders	Approved direction

Step 1: Find Out Who Cares About This Training

Why? So you don't become "road kill" on the e-learning highway. You are starting down a new road. There are all kinds of hazards and areas under construction. The first thing to do is to identify all interested parties so you can be sure to involve them along the way and avoid road blocks later.

These people are frequently called "stakeholders." They are the people who will be affected by your course in one way or another or who want to have a say about some aspect of the course.

Key Point 1: "People support what they create."

Use the following technique based on that Key Point to make your life easier.

Technique 2: How to avoid unnecessary changes:

1. Identify the key players.
2. Include these people all along the way. It will be much harder for them to insist on significant changes later. Get them to take ownership as you progress through your design and development.

Five Principal Stakeholder Groups

At a minimum, consider the following people who might care about or want to have some say in your course.

Let's look at what you might want to know about each of these in more detail.

Sponsor/Requestors/Clients

These are the people who may have asked you to create the course and who can cause you grief if you do not include them in the design. These include the managers of the target audience. If there are many, maybe involve more than one to be sure you are on track. Find out:

- Who will want some say in what the course *contains*?
- Who will want some say in what the course *looks like*?
- Who will be interested in how effective the course is and how they are planning to measure its effectiveness?
- Who will give the approval on the final course design?

Your Boss

Just how much will your boss have to say about the course? The more your boss has to say, the more frequently you want to involve him/her in decisions.

Subject Matter Experts (SMEs)

Who will likely be contributing content to or reviewing the course? What is their availability? Whom do they report to? Can you get the support of their boss so that they know this is something they need to attend to on time?

Target Audience

While it might seem like they have little to say, they can cause a serious accident on that e-learning highway! They can give you insight into what works and what doesn't. Make sure you involve them at some point along the way so you don't get blindsided.

Corporate Departments

There could be one or more corporate departments that have to give their blessing to your course before you go public. These are the common ones but there could be more. If you find any, get commitments regarding how long their reviews will take. They are notorious for causing delays.

- **Communications**: Check with the communications department to see about branding requirements—what colors you can or cannot use, what logos, icons you can or must use or cannot use.
- **Legal:** Check with the legal department to see if they need to review the course content and if so, when.
- **HR:** Check with human resources to see if they have any guidelines you need to adhere to or restrictions. I remember one course with something like a hundred pages, many of which contained photos of people that HR put into a 5-mile long traffic jam. HR decided that there was not enough diversity in the photos. The developers had to spend days replacing the images with people of different ages, sex, and race.

Step 2: Find Out What the Course Sponsor is Trying to Accomplish

Someone wants you to write this course. Talk to them. Ask what they hope to accomplish with this course. What they hope the learners will be able to do after taking the course that they could *not* do before. This is the purpose of your course. Write it down. Laminate it. Tattoo it on your hands. Make it your screen saver. It is your bumper sticker for the e-learning highway. It is your driving force.

Sometimes referred to as the "terminal objective," the course purpose will become your guiding light during the entire design process. Why bother with this? Your boss has said you need to create this course. What more could you need? I am reminded of an old saying that applies here: "*If you don't know where you are going, you will probably end up somewhere else.*" Applied to training this means:

Key Point 2: If you are not very clear about where you want the training to go (its end result), then there is a really good chance that what you achieve will be not be what is needed.

Your training may be good stuff but not the *right* stuff. People may like the way the course looks but down the road they will likely be unhappy with the *results* of the training or worse yet, begin to think that training is useless because they see no changes, which in turn could jeopardize your job.

What Is a Course Purpose?

The course purpose is a broad statement of intent, frequently performance, job, or business related. The course purpose answers the question, "What does your organization hope to accomplish from a business perspective? (Reduce costs? Reduce accidents? Increase sales?) Read over these examples.

Ex: "The purpose of this course is to increase sales of ___ by improving your [sales techniques | product knowledge]."

Ex: "The purpose of this course is to increase productivity by improving managers' skill in coaching employees."

Ex: "The purpose of this course is to decrease accidents by getting workers to adopt safer work habits."

Ex: "The purpose of this course is to increase profits by enabling store owners to manage their inventory better."

For you and for the learner it is the reason the course exists and why people should be paying attention to the content. It has two parts: 1) the business need and 2) how the course satisfies that need.

Course Purpose Dissection

Notice that these are stated in *two-parts*.

- The *first* part is the business/organization need (increase sales, increase productivity, decrease accidents, increase profits). This is the *impact* of the training.

- The *second* part that comes after the word "by" is the desired results of the course (improving sales techniques, improving coaching skill, adopting safer work habits, enabling better inventory management).

The first part of the purpose gives a reason for the second part. The second part is how the course helps achieve the first part. This approach to a course purpose has a motivating effect by showing the *relevance* of the course to the business.

Another way to look at the relationship between the two parts is this.

Two Parts of Course Purpose

Training	Leads to	Second part of purpose: Short-term results	Leads to	First part of purpose: Long-term business impact
Management training	→	Improved managers' skill	→	Increased productivity
New phone features training	→	Improved product knowledge	→	Increased sales
Safety training	→	Safer work habits	→	Decreased accidents and associated costs

In short, *explain how this course will satisfy the business need*. What are the expected behavior changes as a result of taking this course? What are the business benefits?

Have a powerful course purpose written down and keep it in front of you as you write. It will make your course succinct and powerful.

Key Point 3: If you can't write a purpose that connects the course to a business benefit, question the real value of the course.

How to Draft a Powerful Course Purpose

Technique 3: How to draft a powerful course purpose:

1. Jot down at a high level how the learners are expected to change as a result of taking this course.

2. Figure out how the organization is expected to benefit because of this change.

3. Put these together and write your course purpose.

Identify the Business Need for the Course.

If you can't write down a business need, you probably will have a weak course. You won't be able to explain to people why they should learn and apply what is being covered. You won't be able to be sure that you have covered everything necessary to achieve the desired ends.

While this book is about design, not analysis, here is just a little bit about how to analyze the situation. For more on analysis, see the book by Morrison, et. al. listed in the References at the end of this book for extensive coverage of this topic.

Situation Analysis

Start by getting answers to these questions:

- What is the situation? (What is going on?) (Ex. Anti-harassment laws are getting tougher.)
- What is the problem (the gap between what is or would be without this training and what is desired) or what is the opportunity you want to take advantage of? (Ex. People are still being harassed and are filing bigger suits.)
- What is the impact if the problem is not solved or the opportunity is not taken advantage of? (Ex. Large payouts in court.)
- What business functions/jobs/tasks are not being performed or are being performed incorrectly due to lack of training? I.e. what changes are needed?

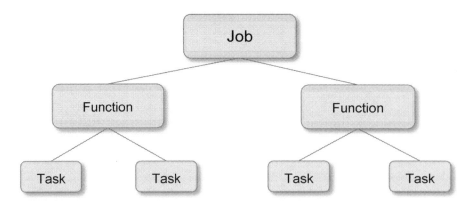

- What evidence is there that the problem is lack of training or is something else the problem such as the work environment, motivation, customer demand, general business climate, etc.?

Tip 3: If you are getting a little stuck, try answering these questions:

What would happen if learners did *not* take this course?

How would the business suffer?

You will likely come up with some things that will not happen but should (sales, productivity) or things that will but should not (accidents, lawsuits, dissatisfied customers).

Take these and reframe them into positive outcomes if the learner *does* take the course. Presto, you have the business half of your course purpose. Then add the second half by stating how the course will address the business need focusing on what the learners will be better able to do at the conclusion of this course.

How to Use a Course Purpose

Best Practice 1: If what you are considering including in the content or doing is not **directly** contributing to the purpose of your course, get rid of it!

That pretty much says it all.

Step 3: **Nail-down Who the Trainees Are**

Find out all you can about your target audience so you can stay learner focused as you develop the course.

Your target audience is the people who are going to take your course—your learners/trainees. Because it can make a big difference in how you design your course, you need to be sure everyone is in agreement as to just who will be taking the course—who needs this knowledge—who needs to improve. You need to know the important characteristics of the learners. These will help you create a learner-centered course. (See *Telling Ain't Training* by Stolovitch and Keeps for excellent coverage of this topic.) And most importantly, this target audience description will help you design a course that has better chances of transferring back to the job and having the desired impact.

Five Types of Essential Information about Your Learners

You will probably find these five types of information (characteristics) about the learners very useful when you design a course. Each type helps shape the course by guiding:

- What content is included
- What level of detail is needed
- What background information is needed
- How long the course will be
- Whether or not audio and video will work
- How text is worded
- How it will be presented
- The design of *meaningful motivational* exercises

Audience Description Information Types

- How to organize the content
- The overall nature of your scenario and its appropriateness to your audience

Starter List of 32 Audience Description Questions

Ahead is a starter list of questions to ask about your learners. Not all will apply to every target audience. Use the ones that seem to apply to your situation. You should also try to think of others. You are looking for things that will help you better tailor the course to your audience as well as anything that could derail a great course.

Demographics

1. How many learners are projected? (If you only have a few, the expense of developing e-learning may not be warranted.)
2. Where are they located?
3. What is their reading level and native language?
4. What cultural differences need to be considered?
5. What is their typical age?
6. What is their management level? (Managers will want courses that get to the point quickly.)
7. Are there any disabilities considerations (seeing, hearing, moving the mouse, or using the keyboard)?

Current Knowledge Base

8. How familiar are they with course area and terminology? That is, are these people novices, people with some experience, or people with lots of experience in the area? The more familiar they are, the more you will need to allow them to skip content they already know.
9. What courses have they already taken?
10. What should they already know or be able to do? (prerequisites)
    - What courses should they have taken before this one?
    - What skills should they already have?
    - What education level will you be expecting?

11. How familiar are they with working on a computer and specifically e-learning?
12. What is their business background? For example, people from government or education transitioning into business may not be familiar with business terms.

Their Motivation

13. What problems are they having in the topic area?
14. What are the organizational expectations of the learners? To what extent are they meeting those expectations?
15. What are their attitudes or interests?
16. What are their reasons for taking this course? (Forced to? Want to?)
17. Does anything about their job depend on how well they do in this course?
18. How interested are they likely to be in this course?
19. What are their current biases and attitudes?
20. What are their expectations of the course?
21. What is their current performance level (if that is relevant)?

Learning Environment

22. What is the expected screen size (resolution in pixels) used by the target learners?
23. What technologies do they have available? (computer speed, connection speed, browser used, printer available, etc.)
24. Are there any technological restrictions like firewalls or limited ability to install software?
25. If your course had an audio component, would that be a problem? Are you sure their computers have sound cards? Would headphones be needed to keep from disturbing others or to hear over background noise?
26. How much time will likely be available for training sessions? In some environments, learners have only 10-15 minutes for a session while in others they have hours.

27. When will learners be taking this course in their career with the company? When hired? When transferred to a job using this information? Yearly?

28. How soon will the information be used? If not right away, consider lots of job aids.

Where the Information Will Be Used – Application Environment

29. *Where and how* will the learners use the information? Is it in the office? In the manufacturing plant? In a sales meeting? On the phone with a client? In a difficult meeting with an employee? What will be the conditions where they will be expected to *apply* what is learned in the course? This is usually very obvious but usually overlooked.

    – Lighting
    – Noise
    – Interruptions
    – Pressure/stress
    – Temperature
    – Clothing
    – Dangers
    – Tools, equipment, machinery, software

30. Will they be able to use job aids? (If not, you may have to include more exercises to be sure the learners learn what they need to.)

31. Does their work require them to be detail oriented like accountants or high-level thinkers like executives?

32. Are they in a people oriented job like counselors or task oriented like programmers or factory workers?

Once you have this information, you now need to evaluate whether or not your learners will be able to handle a scenario-based course. It is not for everyone. For some, you may have to make it considerably simpler than you had anticipated. Think about the target audience and if you can, discuss your ideas for a scenario-based course with another learning professional to be more sure that this approach is appropriate.

Step 4: Define Specifically What They Need To Be Able To Do

Okay, you have your overall direction stated in your course purpose, you know whom the course is for, and you have some information about it. Now it is time to write some specific performance objectives (sometimes called "enabling objectives") to support the purpose. Performance objectives are the things the learner needs to be able to do to achieve the course purpose.

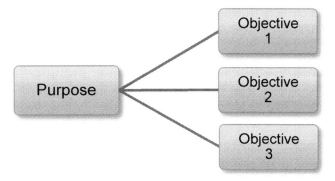

Tip 4: Even if you don't put these in the course, *they are critical to the design* as you will see. Remember, the more concrete you are about what you want the learners to do, the better you can identify what material should be included in the course and what the exercises and most importantly, what your scenario should look like.

Tip 5: Ideally, you should be able to write your performance objectives without gathering any more content. However, many times I have found that I needed to dig into the content more in order to be able to write the objectives. Don't be afraid to do that. Just don't let the availability of content drive your objectives.

Best Practice 2: Use your course purpose to drive your objectives and persist to find the necessary content.

What Is a Performance Objective?

A performance objective is a clear brief statement of what learners should be able to *do* at the conclusion of the course or lesson. Performance objectives deal with target business behaviors or skills necessary to achieve the course purpose(s). Performance objectives do the following:

- **Facilitate course design by identifying the desired end results.**
- **Inform students of the course expectations (motivation).**
- **Serve as guides for selecting appropriate content.**
- **Drive the creation of questions in practice exercises and tests.**

Here is an example.

> Course purpose (from the earlier step):
>> The purpose of this course is to increase sales by improving sales techniques used by customer service representatives.

> Performance objectives for the course: Upon successful completion of this course, the learner will be expected to be able to:
>> – Build rapport with the prospect.
>>
>> – Identify the prospect's interest areas.
>>
>> – Explain the features and benefits of interest to the prospect.
>>
>> – Identify buying signals.
>>
>> – Close the sale.

Guideline 1: For scenario-based training, write goals that involve the learner doing something job related.

What Objectives Are *Not*

Objectives do *not* describe or list what you will *cover* or what will *occur* in the course. That is your agenda or list of course topics or activities. That discussion of what will be covered belongs in the course overview.

Remember, this is "learning by doing" and as such, you should have "doing" objectives that are applicable to the job.

Write Useful Performance Objectives

Technique 4: How to write motivating learner-focused performance objectives:

1. **Begin by asking yourself the key question, "What do the learners need to be able to *do* when they complete the course that they could not do when they began?"** Examine your course purpose and ask what must learners be able to do if they are to achieve it? This is a form of analysis—breaking the goal down into more specific skills and knowledge. *Focus on performance, not on just recall.*

2. Reframe them using action verbs. Eliminate words like "understand" and "know."

3. Make them job-related – Eliminate words like "list "and "describe" because you rarely have to list or describe something on the job.

    Verbs like "list," "define," and "explain" are rarely used on the job. When was the last time your boss asked you to define or list something? Explain – well yes – as in "Explain why this project is late and over budget and no one likes it." See if you can figure out how learners would use the information on the job *to make decisions*. Then rewrite the objectives.

4. Change "you will be able to" to "you will be *expected* to be able to."

Perspective

In most all cases, it is better to state your objectives from an "apply" perspective rather than from a "recall" perspective.

> *"The behavior expressed in an objective should be as real-world as possible and should get away from memory level whenever possible"* (Gibbons & Fairweather, 1998, p. 189).

Job/Task Analysis

In some cases, you may be training people to do part of a job. If so, you may need to perform a job or task analysis to determine what they need to know or be able to do. At a high level, it looks something like this.

- Identify the broad functions performed in the job.
- Break the functions down into tasks and prioritize.
- Break tasks down into steps and guidelines and prioritize.

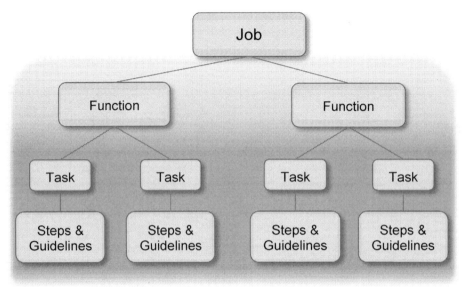

Draw objectives from the darker area

Draw your performance objectives as much as possible from the task level and the steps and guidelines level. This is where the action is. This is the basis for your scenario!

Information Helpful to Writing Objectives

The kind of information you should look for to create your objectives depends on the type of material being taught.

Basis for Objectives

Type of Material Being Taught	Information to Base Objectives On
1. Facts	How would the learner *use* the facts on the job? If they aren't being used, they why are they being taught?
2. Concepts	Examples and non-examples
	What characteristics or attributes make something fit the concept or not? Ex. What is a defect and what is not? What are examples of low, medium, and high severity problems?

Type of Material Being Taught	Information to Base Objectives On
3. Procedures	Inputs
	Transformations, changes, decision points, and indicators
	Outputs and outcomes
	Details of the steps in the procedure
	How to do it
	When to start and stop each step
	What indicators to watch to be sure procedure is on track like timing and quality control issues
	How to make key decisions
	Exceptions
	Cautions
	What might happen if the step is omitted or done wrong
4. Processes	Environment/context/location
	Inputs
	Stages in the process
	Transformations, changes
	Outputs and outcomes
	Exceptions
5. Principles	Examples of cause and effect
	Impacts of not using the principle
	Guidelines for using – when, where, why
	Exceptions
	Cautions

Type of Material Being Taught	Information to Base Objectives On
6. Interpersonal Skills	Key facts or concepts if any
	A model of the key steps in the interaction
	Guidelines for using – when, where, why
	Exceptions
	Cautions
	Impacts of doing it wrong

Tip 6: You can also ask questions like these:

- "What would happen if they did not know this?"
- "What mistakes to new people frequently make?"

Format and Verb Choice

Objectives state what you "expect" that the learner will be able to do. Incorporate that expectation when you state each objective and you automatically add a motivating force to your course. Probably one of the easiest formats to use is:

"After finishing this course you will be *expected* to be able to:"

Follow this by a list of specific actions.

- Use action verbs.
- Also try your best to make them job related. Put yourself in the learner's shoes. Use job-relevant words. Here are a few examples:

Ex: After finishing this course, you will be expected to be able to:

- Complete the ___ form.
- Overcome ___ objections.
- Open a new checking account for a customer.
- Identify safety violations.

Verb Ideas for Objectives from Bloom's Taxonomy

If you want your learners to:	Try verbs like these:
Simply remember previously learned material	arrange, choose, cite, define, distinguish, give an example, group, identify, indicate, label, list, locate, match, name, recite, record, select, state, tabulate
Grasp the meaning of material (comprehend) as shown by translating material from one form to another (words to numbers), by interpreting material (explaining or summarizing), or by predicting consequences or effects.	account for, annotate, associate, calculate, classify, contrast, convert, describe, differentiate, discuss, distinguish, estimate, give examples of, explain, express, extend, generalize, give examples, identify, indicate, interpret, locate, outline, paraphrase, predict, recognize, report, restate (in own words), select, summarize, tell, translate
Use (apply) what was learned (sometimes facts but more often rules, methods, concepts, principles, laws, and theories) in new and concrete situations.	adapt, administer, apply, assess, calculate, categorize, change, chart, choose, classify, collect, complete, compute, construct, contribute, control, demonstrate, determine, develop, discover, experiment, extend, group, illustrate, implement, instruct, predict, project, sequence, show how to, simulate, solve, sort, teach, train, transfer, translate, use, write
Break down evidence (data) into component parts (analyze), identify relationships and understand structural relationships, and draw conclusions by identifying motives and possible causes.	analyze, appraise, break down, calculate, categorize, classify, compare, contrast, correlate, deduce, detect, determine, diagram, differentiate, discover, discriminate, distinguish, divide, examine, experiment, explain, group, interpret, investigate, order, organize, outline, point out, prioritize, probe, question, recognize, relate, research, seeing patterns or trends, select, separate, sequence, solve, subdivide, survey, test

Are Your Objectives "Fuzzy?"

If your objectives do not begin with an action verb that describes an observable behavior, then they are likely "fuzzy" objectives. Let's take a look at some examples:

Examples of Fuzzy, Recall, and Apply Objectives

"Fuzzy" Objective	"Recall" Objective	Better "Apply" Objective
At the conclusion of this course you will:	After finishing this course you will be expected to be able to:	After finishing this course you will be expected to be able to:
Ex: Understand the ___ process.	Ex: List the steps in the ___ process.	Ex: Identify and solve problems with the ___ process. Ex: Use the ___ process to ___.
Ex: Know how to coach an employee.	Ex: State the guidelines for the ___ coaching [sales, supervision …] principle. Ex: List the ___ coaching principles.	Ex: Predict the outcome if the ___ principle is not applied. Ex: Select the best approach to resolving a ___ problem by using the ___ principle.

Best Practices for Writing Objectives

Best Practice 3: *"Start with reality-based learning objectives. **As you design your course, keep reminding yourself of those objectives. That way your WBT [course] will be reality-based as well"*** (Stone & Koskinen, 2002, p. 66).

Best Practice 4: Write course level performance objectives and topic level performance level performance objectives.

Warning 4: Limit each topic (maybe lesson) to three to five objectives.

If you have more, you probably need to rank them. Don't do this alone. Get the project sponsor and SMEs involved. Pick the top ones. Too many objectives will overwhelm the learner.

Test Your Objectives

Training is focused on performing tasks. Tasks are observable (or measurable). Observable objectives ensure that they are related to tasks. Why is that important? We don't get paid for the unobservable. Rarely if ever do we get paid for what we *know*. **We get paid for what we *do*.**

Tip 7: Ask these questions to help ensure you have good objectives.

- ☐ Do they use action verbs?
- ☐ Do the verbs in the objectives consistently use the present tense?
- ☐ Do they specify an observable performance by the learner?
- ☐ Are the objectives directly related to a specific work process, procedure, or content area?

If you want to know more about how to write objectives, see *Making Instruction Work* by Robert F. Mager and *Michael Allen's Guide to e-Learning*.

Do You Really Need Conditions and Criteria/Standards?

Many books suggest you should also include the *conditions* under which the task will be performed along with the *criteria* for satisfactory performance. These are certainly appropriate for in-depth training that involves extensive live training sessions as in sports or firearms training. My personal experience in business is that both the conditions and the criteria are fairly obvious and rarely need to be stated:

- Conditions: Those you find on the job. What others make any sense at all?
- Criteria: Done right! Make the sale, improve performance, perform the skill

Now of course you can be a lot more specific on both, especially the criteria. However, for most e-learning, specifying something like "perform ___ in the ___ environment with a 90% accuracy or success rate" is not applicable because you cannot recreate the environment nor can you measure the accuracy. You simply do not have the ability or resources to impose the conditions or create enough actual practice exercises to determine if the criteria have been met.

That being said, notice that you should already have identified some of the conditions specified when you described your target audience in the topic "Where the Information Will Be Used." Thinking about criteria now might add a bit of focus to your objectives, which may affect the nature and number of practice exercises and your scenario.

Step 5: Review with Key Stakeholders

Best Practice 5: At the end of each task, you should have your design reviewed by the people who care.

By the way, do this *only* if you want to be successful. It will establish early on whether or not you are on track. You can get back on track before you have spent a lot of time working on the wrong things.

Another reason to have your design reviewed early and often is that the more input you allow your stakeholders to have, the more they will support your final product. In this first review, include these people at a minimum.

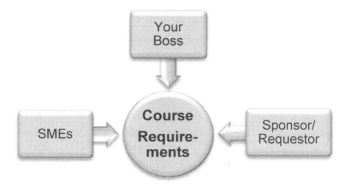

- Make sure your SMEs agree that you have the right objectives and that your questions are addressing the right content.

- Make sure your boss and the project sponsors agree you have the right objectives and have adequately described the audience.

- Ask everyone, "Is there anything else we want people to be able to do after finishing this course?" (I.e. have you missed any important objectives?)

Critical Success Factors

To ensure your success in this task,

make sure you are good with these critical success factors.

Factor	What You Need to Do
1. Clear purpose	✓ **Have a clear course purpose** based on what the sponsor expects from the course.
2. Target audience description	✓ **Know whom the course is for** and that a scenario-based course is appropriate for them.
3. Clear performance objectives	✓ **Have clear *performance* objectives** that describe what the learners need to be able to *do, not* just what they need to know.
4. Approvals	✓ **Review this basis with the stakeholders** before going any further.

Task 2: Collect Your Content

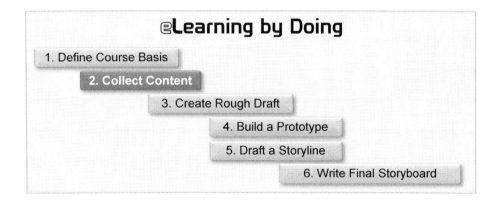

Okay, this is the boring part – collecting the content. This should be very familiar to you if you are an experienced instructional designer. You may refer to it as the Analysis phase in the ADDIE model. What I have tried to do here is start with a little bit of what you know and then add/emphasize the bits that are important for scenario-based e-learning. (If it is not familiar, you should get some training in instructional design before going much farther.)

Steps in This Task

Step	Deliverables
1. Collect basic content	Scraps of paper, notes, files, "war stories"
2. Collect content for the scenario	War stories, cause and effect relationships, clues, cues, and indicators, shades of gray
3. Organize and chunk	Organized content for the presentation portion of the course
4. Review course purpose and objectives	With this new information, you may need to revise the course purpose and objectives
5. Review with stakeholders	Approved content

Step 1: Collect Basic Content

This step covers where to get your source materials and good questions to ask.

Many books and schools tell you to develop your course purpose and instructional objectives *before* you collect information. If you can do this, that is great! More frequently, you will need to know *something* about the topic area *before* you can write goals and objectives.

Interview the project sponsor or requestor and find out why they want this course and what they think it should cover. Have them identify any reference documents you can.

Quickly review any documents on the subject that you can readily lay your hands on. If you can't find enough written material, interview *briefly* some people who do the work and ask them what they need to know to do their job and if they can point you to any more documents. Generally become familiar with the content and who will be using it.

You may simply have a set of new content you are providing to people. If people have ever done anything like this before (sales people learning a new approach or product, managers learning new coaching techniques, training for new hires, etc.) then try to adapt the following questions to learn more about how to communicate the new content to learners and get ready to create stories. Ask:

- "How do the more experienced people do it now?"
- "What do the new people in the job wish they had known earlier?"

Other good sources of scenario like information are:

- Trouble shooting sections of a manual
- What does success look like? Failure?
- What patterns of success or failure appear?
- What are most common problems?
- Where are people likely to make mistakes?
- What are good diagnostic tools (questions)?
- What are timing issues that may make the difference between success and failure?

Best Practice 6: Be sure you have collected data on misconceptions and mistakes to use later when creating obstacles, questions, and question choices.

Tip 8: Know that you will be back here getting more information.

Keep Your Course Purpose and Objectives in Sight

Best Practice 7: Use your objectives as a guide to determine whether or not the information is really needed. Ask, "What is the minimum information the learners need to achieve the objective?" That is what you include in your course.

Review Documents

Begin by reviewing any easily available documents that may shed light on what the learners need to know or be able to do or choose not to do. It puts you in a better position to ask questions of the subject matter experts (SMEs). Here is a list of some of the more common documents to look for:

- ✓ Policy manuals
- ✓ Instruction manuals or guides
- ✓ Government regulations
- ✓ Accident/incident reports
- ✓ Operators guides or handbooks
- ✓ Books
- ✓ A bit of internet research
- ✓ Prerequisite courses if any

Perform a Job/Task Analysis If Needed

- Identify the broad functions performed in the job.
- Break the functions down into tasks and prioritize.
- Break tasks down into steps and guidelines and prioritize.
- Identify the actions needed to perform each step and the supporting knowledge (content/information) required. Document:
    - What the learner needs to do
    - What the learner needs to know
    - What indications to look for to identify when/where to start, when the step is done, and whether or not it has been done right (problems)

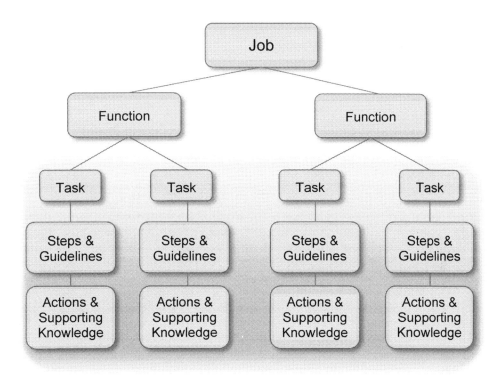

23 Questions to Discover Content Crucial to Your Course

Interviews are a great way to figure out what the learner will need to know. Find a few people who currently do the work you will be training others to do and talk to them. Here is a list of questions to help you in your analysis.

1. How did you learn this?
2. How did you get past the challenging bits?
3. How do you do this task/procedure?
4. What are best practices for ___?
5. What are five case studies, examples, or stories that would help people learn to do this? (Great for exercises)
6. What are some of the typical problems one encounters? (Great for exercises)

7. What are some success tips for a new person on the job?
8. What are the key quality measures?
9. What are the key steps/processes people must follow to do this right?
10. What are the top five things people must know (about this subject, product, system, regulation, issue)?
11. What did you learn recently?
12. What do top performers know or do that novice workers do not? (Clark, 2008b, p. 153).
13. What do you wished you knew on day one?
14. What are some shortcuts?
15. What looks like it should work but does *not*?
16. What does success look like when __ (performance verb—ex. managing, painting)? How do you measure it?
17. What kinds of mistakes are the most costly? Most frequent? Why? How can they be avoided? (Great for exercises)
18. What mistakes did you make at the beginning?
19. What was challenging at first? Why?
20. What would you tell a novice in this area? Why?
21. Where should people go for more help, advice and information on this topic?
22. Why is it done this way? (not always useful)
23. Why is this (step, procedure, whatever) important?

Step 2: **Collect Content for the Scenario**

In addition to your normal content, you will need a little additional information to help you with your scenario – e-learning by doing. In particular you will find these helpful:

- War stories
- Cause and effect relationships
- Clues, cues, and indicators

- Shades of gray

Gather "War Stories"

Best Practice 8: Get those war stories – stories of how people overcame significant (job related) barriers.

War stories are simply stories that involve challenge, overcoming significant obstacles, hardship, danger, etc. They can be about successes or failures. For some reason, failures seem to be more memorable. Perhaps it is because "experience is the best teacher" but in my experience it can be expensive!

Key Point 4: IMPORTANT – making your scenario realistic requires more stories from the SMEs – especially when creating interactions and feedback. Be sure to identify and capture any kind of cause and effect.

Here are a few examples:
- What is the employee doing that is causing low productivity?
- What happens if the supervisor does this? Does that?
- What happens if the worker misses a hazard?

Clark Quinn, one of the best writers on scenario-based learning, writes

> "The key to choosing the appropriate alternate paths comes not from making believable alternative ... but from the misconceptions learners have demonstrated when applying the knowledge. the more likely the misconception is to be exhibited by learners, the more important it is that that option be made available and trapped." (Quinn, 2005)

Generally there are four groups you can gather war stories from.
- **Recent hires** – people who are right now learning from their mistakes and those mistakes are fresh in their minds. They still remember what mistakes they made starting out and what was helpful. Be sure you tap this resource.
- **Inbetweens** -- people who have been around a while but are not yet experts.

- **Experts** – people who have become known for knowing how to do something. Chances are that they have made more mistakes than most other people and will have some good stories to tell.
- **Bosses** -- can tell you about things that worked and will certainly remember those big mistakes made by people reporting to them.

Technique 5: How to collect war story information:

1. Get the following usual info:
   - ✓ Who – especially the position description
   - ✓ What – events as they happened
   - ✓ What – cues were there that were missed
   - ✓ When – under what conditions
   - ✓ Where
2. And be sure to get these pieces:
   - ✓ **Goal** – what were they trying to achieve at the time
   - ✓ **Obstacles** – what was hard to do, what went wrong, problems
   - ✓ **How** – methods/techniques to overcome obstacles, cues that helped to solve the problems

Most war stories involve some kind of mistake.

Technique 6: How to collect information on mistakes for the scenario:

1. Begin with something like "Tell me about some of the mistakes you wish you had avoided."
2. For each mistake:
   - How bad do you think it was?
   - How can you avoid making it in the future?
   - How can you remember not to make it?
   - What do you think an expert would have done?
   - What do you think a co-worker would have done?
   - Why do you think the customer did not buy? (getting the learner to think about cause and effect)

Identify Cause and Effect Relationships

Helping learners see the effects of their actions is really what your training is about. Knowing information is not enough. They have to see how it all fits together if they are going to make better decisions and improve performance.

Guideline 2: While you are gathering the content, look for cause and effect relationships because the interactions in your scenario will be decisions made by the learners.

- What are the effects of good and bad decisions?
    - Immediate/short term
    - Delayed/long term
    - Visible/observable
    - Hidden
- What are the negative outcomes, neutral, somewhat positive, and mostly positive outcomes?
- To what extent do some of the positive outcomes also have negative side effects? How are they best handled?

Look at your content as a system. A causes B causes C causes D … Or, it takes A and B and C to cause D. I had an aunt who went out early one morning to feed the horses. It was still pretty dark but she did not turn on the light – she had lived there for 20 years and knew the way and where to duck the overhanging branches. But Uncle Lou had left a rake on the path because he was going to use it the next day. My aunt stepped on it and seriously hurt her foot. So, which decision was the cause: a) not waiting till it was lighter, b) not turning on the light or getting a flashlight, c) not putting the rake away, d) deciding to own horses?

Guideline 3: The lesson here is that your interactions can go many ways. Be sure you get all the perspectives so you can write realistic ones.

Identify Clues, Cues, and Indicators

One reason adults have fewer driving accidents than teenagers is because they know what to look out for on the road. As you gather your war stories, ask questions like these about what to look for so you can build them into your scenario.

- What told you that was the problem (or going to be a problem)?
- How did you know to start doing that to avoid the crisis?
- What should someone look for to avoid that situation?
- What clued you in to knowing that was the problem?
- How did you know you had stepped in something nasty?

Identify Shades of Gray

Best Practice 9: Be sure to gather content about outcomes. This information will be key to creating real-world feedback and a meaningful scoring system.

Given the same interaction with a salesperson, some customers will continue shopping, some customers will ask a lot more questions, some customers will buy, and still other customers will walk out. When you get a war story, ask questions like "Does that always happen?" or "What else happens?" or "Are the consequences always this severe?"

Step 3: Organize & Chunk Content

In most cases you are going to have to deliver some content somehow. When you do, you will need some organization, structure, or framework to hang your course material on. Do the standard instructional design bits here. Don't just dump it on the learner. Here are a few ideas from my *Designing Effective eLearning* book. See that book for details on how to properly structure content that is primarily facts, concepts, procedures, processes, principles, or interpersonal guidelines.

Best Practice 10: Organize your material around job tasks or steps rather than around product features, theory, or models when possible (Clark, 2008b, p. 184). This makes for greater interest and transfer to the job.

When that is not possible, then here are some ideas to organize your course to get you rolling:

- Situation > Problem > Impact > Need
  - Situation: People are eating healthier.
  - Problem: We aren't selling as many burgers and French fries.
  - Impact: Business is down and may have to lay people off.
  - Need: We need healthier food offerings.
- Simple to complex
- Chronological – time-line – before, during, after
- Familiarity – more familiar things first
- Interest – cover the more interesting topics first
- Problem > diagnosis techniques > causes > prevention or solution

Step 4: Review and Revise Course Purpose and Objectives

Tip 9: Now that you have a better feel for the depth of the information you will be covering, review your performance objectives and be sure they cover the content you have identified. You may need to:

- Delete some objectives
- Reword some objectives
- Add some objectives
- Delete some of your content

In either case, it is best to do this now before you get too far down the road. Doing this simple step will save you a lot of time.

Once you have done that, check your course purpose and be sure it is still accurate. What have you learned that may change that purpose?

Step 5: **Review with Major Stakeholders**

The key reviewers in this task are your SMEs. You want them to make sure you have covered the key points. Try to include at least one manager of potential learners. It is a lot easier to change an outline than it is to change a full-blown storyboard and sometimes it can save you lots of work.

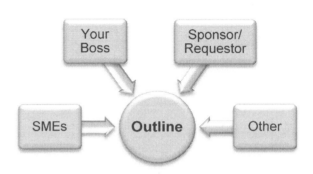

Critical Success Factors

To ensure your success in this task,

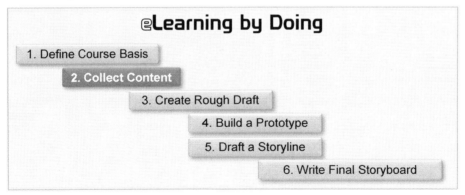

make sure you are good with these critical success factors.

Factor	What You Need to Do
1. Iteration	✓ **Make more than one pass to collect your content.** Get a good sampling and then review your objectives to make sure you are on the right track. Then go back and get more.
2. Having a real basis for the scenario	✓ **Be sure to gather plenty of "war stories"** so you can create realistic interactions and give real-world feedback.

Task 3: Create a Rough Draft

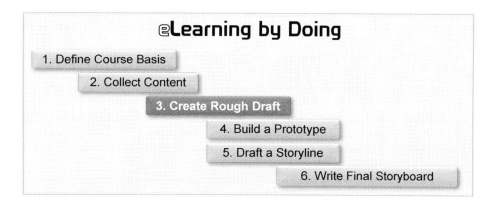

What's Going on Here?

Okay, you've got your content. Now what? Scary stuff! But not if you have this book.

Well, now you need to take a stab at the design and create a rough draft. You use this draft to create a working prototype and a storyline, if there is one. Then you expand this rough draft into your final storyboard. The reason you bother with a rough draft is because it affects the technical design in the authoring tool as well as the storyline. All three interact and you would hate to spend a ton of time on the storyboard only to find that it could not be done easily in your authoring tool or not work with your storyline. You will likely make lots of revisions as you go along.

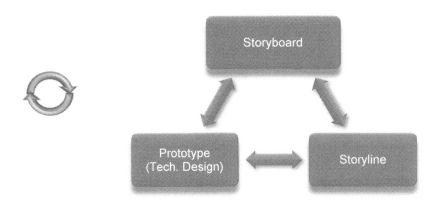

Once you have the rough draft in place, the next task is to build a prototype to test out your design before you have put a lot of work into it. Frequently you will find there are technological limitations you had not expected or things either cannot be done as easily as expected or not at all with the authoring tool you have selected. Sometimes you will discover you will need to make any of a number of changes to your design to make it work as desired and within budget.

What We Are Trying To Do

Remember the sections of an e-learning course that incorporates a scenario that we saw near the beginning of this book? In this task we will create our first cut of this.

Sections of a Scenario Course

Section	Contents/Components
1. Opening Pages	Welcome, introduction, objectives, benefits, set the stage pages
2. Content	Abbreviated content as some should be delivered within the scenario

Section	Contents/Components	
3. Scenario	Opening	Scenario challenge, interface/ navigation instructions page(s), learner customization page(s) if any
	Interaction Segments	Interactions where learners make decisions (usually questions but not always) and get feedback
	Results	Summary of how they did with as much analysis as possible and Debriefing
4. Wrap-up	In longer, more complex courses or scenarios, there may be a separate wrap-up section.	
5. Support	Popup pages containing any kind of support material used by learners	

How to Do It

The following steps to create a rough draft of the above structure are covered in depth in this chapter.

Steps to Create a Rough Draft

Step	Deliverables
1. Describe your overall approach to content delivery	A brief description of *how* you are going to deliver your content, the scenario approach, and how the two will be connected
2. Draft the scenario opening	Description of the scenario portion – the situation and challenge
3. Plan interactions	Brief description of typical interactions for use in building the prototype

Step	Deliverables
4. Draft scoring method	Description of how learners will know how well they did and how they will learn from their mistakes
5. Make media decisions	Proposed media choices
6. Draft interface	Brief description of the prototype, enough so one can be built
7. Review with stakeholders	Approved approach

Step 1: Briefly Outline How You Are Going to Deliver Your Content

Tip 10: When you attempt a scenario-driven approach, a big concern will be how you are going to deliver your content. Here are a few ways to do this:

- Simply have a content section before the scenario as shown in the previous structure.
- Share some information as you set the stage for the decision-making.
- Provide information as part of the feedback.
- Create some ways for the learner to get additional help to answer the question. For example, suggest they check the policy manual or the procedure guide using a link or button.

See *Designing Effective eLearning* by Ben Pitman from Amazon if you need more on how to organize and present content for e-learning. It is a good deal different than for classroom training.

Warning 5: Don't deliver too much content before having the learner use it.

Here is one of my favorite quotes.

> *"Presenting a lot of content that has no chance of affecting behavior (or even being recalled a few days after training) can never be cost-effective, period. It's a waste of money and a lot of time. With all apologies, no matter how politically correct and popular it may be, it remains a stupid thing to do."* (Allen, 2003, p. 227)

I think Michel Allen nailed it there. I have a free paper out, available now on my e-store, entitled "The Biggest Training Mistake." Simply put it is information overload. Most people can remember a 7-digit phone number but if you put those same 7 digits at the beginning of a 20 digit number, most people *cannot get even the first 7*.

Best Practice 11: Limit the amount of content you deliver, especially with a scenario. You want the learner to get involved quickly with applying the content. You can add other "lessons learned" along the way.

If bosses, sponsors, or SMEs keep wanting to include more content, ask them what the impact of information overload is? **Giving too much information runs the risk of the learner *less* not more!**

Step 2: Draft a Great Scenario Opening

This is where your scenario starts. Having a powerful beginning will draw learners into the scenario and increase motivation. A great beginning answers these questions.

- What is the situation? Where? When? How did they get there?
- What is going on?
- What are we trying to do or accomplish?
- What resources are available?
- What kinds of decisions will learners have to make?

From the beginning, you need to prep learners for what is coming. In doing so you will create a "need to know" in the learners minds. Here is one framework to help you get a good solid handle on this. Essentially, it will describe a scenario that requires the learner to know the content in order to resolve the situation.

Technique 7: How to write a great scenario beginning:

1. Identify the situation.
2. Clarify exactly what the problem is.
3. Project what the impact will be if the problem is not solved.
4. Specify what is needed to solve the problem.

Components of a Great Beginning

Components	Description	Examples
1. Situation/ Setting	The current context or environment. A "what where when how" description.	Your office on some typical working day A customer walks into the store … People are getting more health conscious. Your restaurant does not offer many healthy dishes. You run an automobile repair shop. A customer walks into the office.
2. Problem	The gap between what is and what is desired. This is sometimes called the "trigger event."	Two employees are fighting. The customer does not have satisfactory cell phone plan or is looking for a new phone People are going elsewhere for lunch. The customer's car is going clunk clunk.

Components	Description	Examples
3. Impact	What the impact will be if the problem is not solved.	Someone could get hurt.
		The customer could elect another carrier.
		You will continue to lose revenue and could go out of business.
		They will not be able to drive their car.
4. Need	What needs to be done. This will be reworded to be the challenge or goal presented to the learner.	Your goal is to settle the argument and get the office back to work.
		Your challenge is to find a plan that will fill the customer's needs.
		Your goal is to figure out what dishes you could offer.
		Your goal is to diagnose the problem as quickly as possible.

Guideline 4: Take these aspects (situation, problem, impact, need) and draft the opening to your scenario. You can use:

- Documents, charts, graphs, audio recordings, video clips, simple text, and more.

  Videos can be especially powerful in opening a scenario. A clip of a manager talking to the learner explaining the situation, the challenge, and what their goal is can be especially powerful for a kickoff. Once you have an approximate script, you can record a high-quality video with today's smart phones like the Samsung Galaxy. (Cliff Perry, personal email, 2013.)

- Obstacles/Problems between current and desired states of affairs. These will be fleshed out into the interactions in the scenario.

- Characters including the role the learner will take (first person or advisor)

Guideline 5: You know you are done with this when you have described the circumstances that will allow learners to see that the content is important and give them the opportunity to use the content.

Here is a bit more about each of these components. Use those "war stories" you collected earlier as a basis for this part.

Sketch Out the Situation/Environment

Describe the setting for your scenario. Make it as work related if at all possible to enhance transfer to the job – store, call center, office, restaurant, meeting, work site …

Think something like "You are [in the office, plant, on the job site, at the reception desk …]

A good environment is crucial to transfer back to the job. You still can have some fun with it though.

Sketch Out the Problem and Impact

Now, what is the problem there?

- Some kind of an impending disaster?
- The money doesn't add up?
- Your first day on the job and you have not sold a thing yet?

Come up with a crisis that will give you grounds for a good goal.

Ex: "It is (time) in (location). You … (situation). So, your job will be to … Before you start, your boss/coach/whoever has a quick briefing for you on …"

Write down briefly what is going on now that could be causing a crisis. You can include here or in the environment information sources such as management manuals, memory joggers, job aids, questions that can be asked, etc.

But it is not enough just to have a problem if it does not relate to the learner.

Guideline 6: You need the "Impact" aspect to help create your storyline, a sense of urgency, and possibly help you word the results section of the scenario.

The impact is the long term and short term consequences if the problem is not solved. From those "war stories" use:

- Immediate/short term results
- Delayed/long term outcomes
- Visible/observable outcomes
- Hidden outcomes

Sketch Out the Need (Challenge/Goal)

Draft what goal you want the learner to achieve in the scenario. Not the performance objectives or the course purpose, but something like sell ___, increase production to ___, win that work contest ___, get a promotion ___. Essentially resolving the current situation. Don't spend a lot of time on the wording as it will likely change.

Select Your Scenario Approach

Based on the course purpose, come up with a couple of alternate approaches to run by your team or someone. In simply talking through your alternatives, you may find that some are better than others. For some reason, explaining your ideas to someone else is frequently a lot quicker than trying to compare them by yourself.

How will the situation unfold, change, develop as learners progress? What kinds of decisions will learners make? Do the surroundings need to change?

Scenario Approaches

Approach	Description	Frequently Used With
1. Linear	One scene after another, usually on separate pages or slides Usually used where each scene calls for different graphics	Interpersonal skills, sales, supervision, coaching, procedures, processes

Approach	Description	Frequently Used With
2. Branching	Each scene can lead to one of several other scenes	Interpersonal skills, sales, supervision, coaching, procedures, processes
3. Active Objects	A very limited number of pages, frequently just one, where the learner clicks on objects on the page to make decisions or gather information – anything where most of the interactions can take place with a fixed set of objects that the user can click on or select	Diagnosis (automobile, emergency room), evaluation, assessment, analysis

Write a Story Summary If Needed

If your scenario involves interpersonal interactions like selling, coaching, supervision, then it may require a storyline. It is too early to write the entire story but you should write a story summary – essentially what happens after the opening scene – how the scenario unfolds. Include:

1. Context/Setting /Environment/ Surroundings	•	Where and when this takes place. The description here will be used to create graphics.
	•	Can include initial character descriptions
2. Situation/ Trigger Event(s)	•	What is happening now, current circumstances, conditions, or as Clark (2013) says on p. 65, the trigger event. At times, you may need provide additional information to the learner ("case data" Clark p. 66). For some scenarios, this may be all that is needed. For others, there may need to be more.

Step 3: **Plan the Interactions**

Once you have an overall approach to the scenario, it is time to plan how your learners will be interacting with your scenario. Here your goal is to describe the kinds of decisions the learner will be making so you can:

- Be sure they will work by piloting them in your prototype in the next task
- Be sure your stakeholders agree that you are taking an acceptable approach

In our planning, you need to describe not only some typical interactions but also how the learner will get guidance or support and how branching will work if any.

Describe Typical Interactions

This is where the "learning by doing" comes in.

Begin by writing a brief description of several typical interactions. Include these components:

- The **setting or situation**
- The **decision** to be made (question)
- **Support** resources learners may want to draw on to help them make the decision (manuals, guides, summary tables, popup windows, etc.)
- The **choices** they have
- How the learner will indicate their choice (check boxes, radio buttons, clicking on hot spots, selecting from dropdown menus, etc.)
- **Feedback** for the choices which may include observable outcomes, hidden outcomes, relevant content, scoring (points, dollars, changes in dials, gauges, meters, etc.)
- What happens next (especially relevant for a branching scenario)

Let's look at these in more depth.

Describe the Situation

Consider using more than just text to present the situation (question) to learners. Make sure whatever you use, the learner can come back and review it easily later if they want to. Consider using a variety of ways to describe the situation (situation descriptors) including:

- Text
- Pictures, diagrams, maps
- Audio
- Video
- Animation
- Meters/gauges for things visible or not visible like customer mood

Describe Typical Decisions

Once you have presented the situation to learners, they will need to make a decision and indicate their choice.

Key Point 5: *"The key to the design of process exercises for employees involved in problem solving is to collect realistic case studies of common malfunctions, customer questions, and so forth that can be converted into practice exercises. "Clark*, 2008b, p. 13.

What Clark has to say about regular courses applies even more so to scenarios.

Guideline 7: Start with your performance objectives. Using them as a guide, make a list of the kinds of decisions learners need to make. Without worrying too much about the interface, draft a list of the decisions the learner should make (questions the learner should be able to answer).

Here are the most effective classes of decisions. Whatever you choose, look for ways to make the method as close to reality as possible.

Decision Classes

Class	Example
1. Explanation	Learners are asked to explain to *someone* why the employee/prospect/system reacted this way.
	Ex: From a coaching course: "In order to boost productivity you set new goals for all your team members. After a week, you still see no improvement. Your boss calls you into his office and asks for an explanation. What would you say"
2. Prediction	Learners are asked to predict what will happen next. It is important to keep it in context with the scenario.
	Ex: "One of your teammates has suggested the team do ____. As you give your response, you outline what would be the most likely outcome/result/impact if the team takes that course of action. What would you say?"
3. Action	Learners are given a situation and asked to decide what they would do.
	Ex: "The situation is ___. What would you do?" or "How would you take care of this?"
4. Diagnosis	Learners select a way to get more information from a list or by clicking on something.
	Ex: "Which question would you ask the customer to uncover her objection?"
	Ex: "What test would you run to find out the most valuable information?"
5. Calculation	Learners are asked to do some math and enter their answer in a box.
	Ex: "With the changes you just made, calculate the new tax amount."

Class	Example
6. Coding/ Rating	Learners are being trained in some terminology, coding, or rating scheme. The questions would give them a situation and ask for their response. Ex: "Given the insurance claim above, what would your diagnosis code be?" Ex: "How would you rate this deficiency?"

Select the Most Likely Computer Question Types

Remember your goal here is to make sure the authoring software can do it and the stakeholders get a fair idea of what these will look like in the scenario. So, once you have several typical decisions outlined, use the next table and for each type of decision, select the appropriate method.

Decision to Computer Question Type

Decision	Computer Question Type
1. Selecting from a list of choices (text or graphics) –	Multiple choice (selecting *one* choice from a list) or Multiple response (check all that apply)
2. Rating items along a single scale	Drag and drop Ordinal rating Slider bar
3. Categorizing or classifying items	Drag and drop (best) Compound multiple-choice single answer (1 for each item)

Step 3: Plan the Interactions

Decision	Computer Question Type
4. Identifying areas to be investigated, the main cause of a problem, the outcome of a situation, or action to take	Multiple-choice Static or dropdown list/menu Hotspots on a map, picture, or diagram Click on an object
5. Arranging things in sequence such as process steps, along a timeline, or order of importance	Drag and drop
6. Teaching the correct placement of items such as furniture or equipment	Drag and drop
7. Labeling a diagram or map	Drag and drop Matching Several fill-in-the-blank questions with the entry boxes near the point on the diagram or map Several multiple choice questions using a dropdown lists
8. Estimating/calculating an amount	Fill-in-the-blank (best) Multiple-choice single answer Slider bar
9. Entering the right code	Fill-in-the-blank (best) Multiple-choice single answer

Warning 6: Limit the number of different types of questions you use. While it may be fun to use different types, each time learners encounter a different type, they have to think a little about what to do rather than stay in the scenario. If you use just one or two types, how to answer the question will fall into the background and they will be able to focus on the scenario.

Feedback Style

To be sure everyone is on the same page about what the feedback will look like, write and describe some feedback for each of your typical exercises.

Guideline 8: Give some examples of feedback for the typical interactions you created earlier. You will need these for your prototype and to give stakeholders an idea of what to expect.

Guideline 9: Specify how the feedback is to be displayed. Is it going to be a popup window, a change in character expression, dials or gauges changing, etc.

Guideline 10: Try to focus on the consequences of each choice.

Ex: "The car fails to start." "The customer walks out." "Productivity does not improve."

Guideline 11: Provide a way for learners to access more information like a "Why" button. This allows you to expand on the course content.

Decide on Instruction/Guidance Options

Not all scenarios will lend themselves to all of these guidance options. This covers much the same ground as how you are going to deliver you content except here you are focusing on:

- What kind of assistance you will make available *at the time learners make decisions* and
- What kind of guidance you provide *after* making a less than optimal choice.

Step 3: Plan the Interactions

Instruction/Guidance Options

Option	Description
1. On-demand content	Buttons or menus that open support documents such as manuals, reference documents, policies, pocket guides, websites, etc.
2. Feedback	What is displayed or what happens after a choice/decision is made by the learner
3. Hints/Coaching from Advisors	When incorrect decisions are made, have a relevant expert (manager, acknowledged expert, senior team member) provide advice for the next try.
4. Multiple tries	In some situations, you can simply allow learners to keep trying until they get it right. Be sure not to frustrate them.
5. Faded Support	• Explore/Demo followed by • Partially worked mode with hints followed by • One with no hints

Your scenario may call for one or more of these things. Look for ways you can incorporate them into your scenario that is natural – realistic in the workplace. Depending on your scenario, you may want to make them available at any time or just at certain times.

- (Library, Documentation, Policies and Procedures, xxx User Guide, ... Manager's Handbook, ...
- Description of the sales process – best put in the form of a real job aid
- Description of principles involved– best put in the form of a real job aid
- Analysis tools like calculators, spreadsheets
- Charts, graphs, diagrams– best put in the form of a real job aid
- Forms
- Glossary – maybe you can turn this into a dictionary or words from an expert
- Job aids

- Tips – possible position as memos or emails
- Questions to ask – possible position as memos or emails
- Briefings (1-2 pages of info) – possible position as memos or emails
- Examples

Design Branching

Branching provides learners with a sense of their own freedom which makes the scenario more believable, interesting, compelling and effective. Each time the learner has an opportunity to change the sequence of the events, it is a *decision point*. At each of these points, the learner makes a choice regarding the direction of the course.

Warning 7: If you decide to use some type of branching, be prepared for testing to take considerably more time.

Types of branching

Branching comes in two fundamental types. Think about using both types to give more interest to your scenario.

- Configuration branching – Choices/decisions that are focused on where they want to start, the level of difficulty, how they want to customize the course, etc. The choices that are *not* focused directly on overcoming an obstacle (solving a problem). Usually they are *not* focused on the content. Their main intent is to give the learner a sense of freedom/control over the experience. Here are just a few examples.

    Ex: "Which management technique do you want to try first?"

    Ex: "Do you want to try a hard customer or easy one first?"

    Ex: "Click where you want to start in the plant."

    Ex: "Click the difficulty level you wish to start with?"

    Another use for these questions would be at the beginning to help you and the learner determine which parts of the course are appropriate.

    Ex: "Check the management courses you have already completed."

    Ex: "Enter the number of months of experience you have in ___."

- Storyline branching (true decision points) – Choices/decisions that occur as a result of choosing an action to overcome an obstacle – you missed identifying a hazard, how you worked with an employee, what you said to a customer.

    Ex: "Click the part you want to fix next or click the Return to Customer button." If the learner clicks this, they are indicating that they think they are through and you can now evaluate performance – maybe by having another worker test drive the vehicle or an irate customer.

Diagramming

A diagram maps the branching to take place. It is composed of a series of decision nodes, panels, screens, scenes, states, events, or steps. *You do not always need one.* It is probably best developed in Excel or Visio although I have seen special tools for this. Personally, I use Excel because I am familiar with Microsoft drawing tools and I can have a diagram that exceeds one page in width and yet see it all on the screen. I use connectors to connect the boxes. Very easy.

Essentially there are two basic forms:

1. Tree or organization chart form and
2. Spider web (a very simple one for us)

This first example is one of a straight branching. The learner makes a choice and then, after feedback, ends up at one of three scenes. There they make another choice and get feedback but there is no real choice. They are simply end up at the next common scene. The fact that they have no real choice (that all end up at the same scene) is not obvious to the learner.

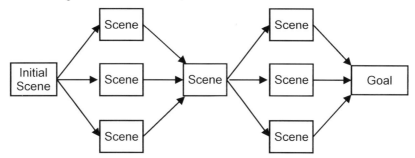

In this example, sometimes referred to as a tree diagram, the user has many paths through the course.

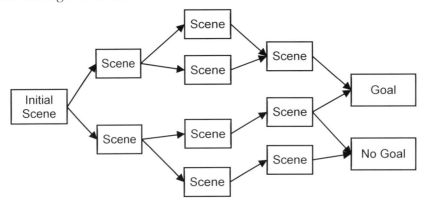

This next one is the basis for spider web branching. The learner can go and come back to the same point.

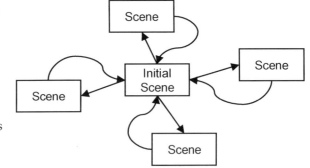

- One example might be that the learner has four employees and can work with any one of them on a given day. After feedback, they are returned to the central point for the next day where now they can choose to work with any employee, including the one from yesterday.

- Another example is diagnosis and treatment. In the Initial Scene then select a test to run or a. The scenario branches to performing that test and getting the results. Then it returns to the Initial Scene with somehow the results of the test or treatment incorporated. For example, the car now starts but won't stay running or the patient can breathe easier but now complains of a headache.

A diagram like the one shown is not hard to build. It can be hooked together with others to build a more complex structure.

Implementation

You can put into branching action using:

- Multiple choice questions
- Fill in the blank questions
- Clicking on buttons or even
- Drag and drop
    - Drag the steps into a particular and then process the scenes in that order
    - Drag an employee into an office and that starts the dialog

Help the Learner Make a Decision

You can also provide buttons near the navigation decision points that provide additional information in a form like "Can't decide? Click here."

Things to Exclude

If you find that you have a need for the following or things like them, they are best put outside the context of the scenario to help maintain fidelity to the real world.

- Licensing agreement
- About this course
- Course objectives
- Email for help

Once you have the first draft of the scenario, you may want to consider making different modes available to the learner. At least one author suggested that different modes be made available. Captivate® does something like this for helping people learn software.

Step 4: Draft Scoring, Results, and Debriefing Approach

You need to think about scoring, presenting the results, and debriefing now as they will have a significant effect on your design. Knowing what you are going to present the learner with at the *end* enables you to collect the necessary information along the way. It is also key to developing the prototype. You want to be sure that your scoring ideas are implementable.

First, don't have scoring just for scoring sake. Remember you are striving for a scenario that is similar to the workplace. Using stars for a score would be *not* be appropriate unless there was some kind of scoring going on in the departments that currently used stars. You are better off using the performance measures the departments might be measured on: number of accidents, number of sales, productivity, etc.

Another alternative would be to use something like the number of hazards identified even though the department does not keep track of them. It does make it into a game but doing otherwise might make it difficult to design. A better way might be to go for zero safety violations and each one missed runs the meter up instead of down. The learner's goal would be to go for a low score (like golf) rather than a high one.

Start with the course purpose and the scenario goal. Then:

- **Design some kind of scoring system that will enable you to determine if the learners achieved the scenario goal.**
- **Sketch out how you will present the extent to which the learner reached the goal.**
- **Sketch out how you will debrief learners to maximize what they get from the course.**

Scoring

Best Practice 12: Try to design a scoring system that gives more information than just passed or failed. Most learners will master some parts of the content but not others. A good scoring system tells the learner what areas they need to review.

I recently did a scenario for a hotel chain that was training the people who went around and made sure the hotels were up to standard. They were shown pictures of a deficiency and asked to rate it. They had to select the correct category (clean, repair, replace, others) as well as the level of severity (low, medium, high). The scoring at the end of the scenario reflected

- How many they had selected with the *incorrect* category
- How many they rated the right category but were too high
- How many the rated too low

Here are a few ideas to get you started. Keep an overall score that could be represented by:

- number of sales, accidents, etc.
- value of sales,
- likelihood of something happening (customer buying a phone)
- production
- attitude

Show these using:

- some kind of dial or meter
- progress bar
- partially completed form
- stacks of what was produced

Guideline 12: If there is natural scoring method or way of measuring performance in the nature of your scenario, use the performance objectives. Summarize how learners did for each objective.

Warning 8: Avoid using things like collecting tokens or earning points unless you do that in the workplace. Remember – Transfer to the job is key.

Shades of Gray

Best Practice 13: Design your scoring so that learners earn more for better answers because this reflects the fact that the real world is not black and white but rather shades of gray.

Simpler scenarios have only one right answer or conclusion. Good scoring reflects shades of gray by awarding different points for different answers rather than points or no points. Feedback reflects this by using different wording.

Limitations of the Authoring Tool

This is one of the few times that you need to consider the limitations of the authoring tool. For example, creating bar charts may be easy but creating line graphs (typically used in sales) may not. This is one of the main reasons you want to build a prototype – to be sure what you want to do can be done without going to a lot of effort. Remember, we are trying to keep costs down.

Debriefing

In a classroom course you might have a coach or facilitator go over the results of the scenario/role-play/simulation and help you learn from it. Another word for this is "process" the results of the simulation. If you cannot provide an instructor to do this after the course, then draft some questions you want learners to think about to help them do a better job next time.

- Debriefing allows the learner to provide the judgment which frequently is remembered longer.
- Debriefing allows the learner to take different perspectives on the situations.
- Debriefing provides more opportunity for the learner to see cause and effect.

It is more than just telling the learner what they did wrong. It attempts to help them figure that out for themselves. It allows them to reflect on their performance and think about next steps. Try free entry questions like these:

- Why do you think you did not make the sale / improve production?

- What caused sales/production to go down?
- What principles to you think you need to understand better?
- How could you remember the ___ better>
- What caused you to get such a low score?
- What was the biggest lesson you learned from this exercise?
- What areas do you need to review before you try this scenario again?

In this task, just consider whether or not debriefing makes any sense for your scenario. If so, jot down a few ideas. You will flesh these out when you write the final storyboard.

Step 5: **Make Strategic Decisions Regarding Media**

With regard to animation, audio, and video, Michel Allen cited Lowe who warned:

> *"animation can overwhelm learners by presenting complex information too fast and in a format that prohibits needed parsing and exploration. It can underwhelm learners leaving them to think they fully understand something they have only seen and insufficiently engaged to really use."* (Lowe 2004, p. 558 in Allen, 2007, p. 163.)

You may have lots of ideas about what you can do here. Just make notes knowing that audio, animation, and video add considerable cost to the scenario that do not necessarily match their contribution to the learning. Make the final decision when you write the storyboard.

Step 6: **Draft the Interface**

The nature of the interface (what it will look like on the screen) is one of the most important things you will do. Write a brief description of the interface the user will see – i.e. what the prototype should look like. It should include example decisions to be made and feedback to make sure things will work as planned and that the stakeholders do not find any issues with your design.

- How will learners be presented with challenges?
- How will they make their choices?
- How will learners find out more about the situation/challenge in order to make a decision? I.e. get more information for the action choice, diagnosis, assessment, analysis, evaluation?
- How will content be delivered or made available? How will they obtain guidance and support and instruction?
- How will they get feedback? Feedback – reflection of the effectiveness of the learner's action -- consequences
- How will then know overall how they are doing? – score
- How will they have an opportunity to reflect on their performance (debrief)? (Clark, 2013, p. 42)

One way to make the course a little more meaningful to learners is to use their name, particularly on the Welcome and Congratulations pages. If you are going to pull the student name from your LMS or have learners enter it, create sample pages that use this technology. Many LMSs give the name as "last name, first name." If this is the case, you should find some way to reverse it before displaying on the screen. Consider using only the first name to make it more personal.

Draft the Navigation

Design not only how the learner will move around but also how they will have access to information sources including the content. Again, you want to be sure your ideas are implementable in the authoring tool.

Draft Learner Customization

Look for ways to personalize the scenario to the current learner. Here are some ideas I have used along the way.

- Using the learner's name (entered on the first page and retained if restarted)
- Male/female pictures for the boss
- Male/female pictures for themselves

- Transcript on/off
- Sound on/off when it was not critical to the learning
- Different background pictures (one for an office and one for a store depending on where the sales person was located)
- Allowing the learner to select which of aspects of the multiple levels they want to include or exclude
- Allowing them to name to the characters
- Allowing them to specify their level of expertise which could control:
  - Question difficulty
  - Hints
  - Resources available
  - Whether or not they have a Back button

Specify the Nature of the Interactions

For the exercises and scenario interactions you need to provide the developer who is converting your storyboard to something that can be viewed online with:

- Instructions
- Number of questions per page

You should also describe some technical consideration of how the interactions should behave.

Behavior Considerations of Interactions

Consideration	Description/Explanation
1. Required or not	Are learners required to answer the question before continuing?
2. Answer weight	How many points will be given for each answer choice?

Consideration	Description/Explanation
3. Feedback display method	Whatever feedback you give, if you can, display it in the same window as the question and do it so that the question and relevant answer choices are still visible rather than using a popup window. It makes it easier for the learner to associate the feedback with the chosen answer *and* it is easier to show the feedback if the learner returns to the page later.
4. Feedback display timing	You can have the question give feedback as soon as they select an answer or you can allow them to change their answer before committing by clicking on a button.
5. Check Answer button	Name the button something like "See what happened" instead of "~~Check My Answer~~" or "~~Submit~~" because it helps learners stay in the scenario.
6. Indication of the correct answer	The feedback should indicate the optimal choice answer at some point, but maybe not on the first try.
	Additionally, consider showing a red X next to any incorrect answer that was selected and possibly a green checkmark (✓) next to the correct answer(s).
7. Hints	If you have allowed multiple tries, it is sometimes useful to provide hints to the learners if they did not get the question correct. These can take the form of information or referring the learner to some other part of the course or other reference material. You can have these appear after the first incorrect try or have a Hints button that appears so that learners can keep trying on their own if they want to.

Consideration	Description/Explanation
8. Changing their answer	If, after answering the question and getting some feedback, are they allowed to change their answer? That might be okay if your feedback did not specify the correct answer but just gave instructional and real-world feedback. Then they could continue to try the practice exercise several times to see what would happen for the other choices. However, don't let them go on too long without giving them the correct answer. Remember, people need to learn here as well as when reading the content.
	If you do not want to allow them to change their answer, you may have to do something to keep them from changing their answer. Frequently this is accomplished by showing a transparent rectangle or button that covers the answer choices to prevent learners from changing their answer. Some software can gray-out the choice buttons.
9. Behavior if the learner returns to the exercise	If they answered it correctly, will they be required to complete the exercise again? (Not recommended.) Instead, immediately enable the Next button.
	If they answered it incorrectly the first time, then do not show just an incorrect answer choice without feedback because this might be misread as being the correct answer. So what can you do?
	• Show their current incorrect choice along with its feedback. This is easy to do if the feedback text is embedded on the page but not so easy if the feedback is a popup window. If you take this route, can they try the question again?
	• Reset the question to unanswered so they must try it again.
	If you don't want to allow them to change their answer, you may have to do something special as discussed earlier.

Consideration	Description/Explanation
10. Limiting the number of tries the learner can have	Allowing more than just one try encourages the learner to experiment and learn even more. Use this for practice exercises but not for games and tests. Unless the route to a correct answer is easy, do not force learners to keep trying until they get the correct answer. Instead, give them two or three tries and then show the correct answer.
11. Behavior if the learner exhausts all tries	Practice exercises should provide some way for learners to see the correct answer. Either: • Simply show the correct answer or • Show a button that will display the correct answer and allow them to continue trying. Use a button that says "Show Answer" which makes it very clear what is going on.
12. Retaining answers between sessions	If the learner quits the course in the middle, when they return, will it react as a continuation of the previous session?

It is not hard to exceed the limits of an LMS to store answers from a previous session because some software stores the entire answer choice (a full sentence) rather than just one character indicating the answer choice. To minimize the amount of data that needs to be stored you can apply the next two tips.

Tip 11: Use variable names that are as short as possible. Example: Q1 instead of Question_0001.

Tip 12: Use answer choices as short as possible. Example: "A" instead of "A. Lecture the employee on the impact of being late." You can hide these internal answers and show the learner the full text of the choices in a block of text. It takes more work to set this up, but once done for one question you should be able to copy and paste the question and change the text. (Beware: If your authoring tool assessment results page shows the choices or answers, you may not want to use this technique as "A" will not mean much to the learner at that point.)

Outline the Scoring

- Specify what will be needed to support the scoring analysis at the end of the scenario.
- Outline what you will want to see on the results page(s).
  - What the overall score was
  - Some analysis/breakdown to help them figure out where they went wrong
  - Text describing the impact of their performance (good and bad)

    Ex: "Your production looks like it is going up/down due to your coaching efforts."

    Ex: "You did not sell enough ___ to meet your quota."

    Ex: "Looks like you learned enough to safely operate a ___."
  - Text describing what they should do next

Step 7: Review with Stakeholders

It is very important to run your rough draft by the course sponsor and a typical learner and see what they think. Have a list of questions to ask them like these:

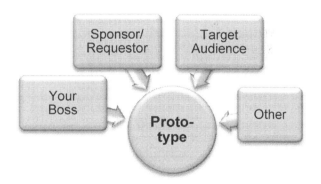

Stakeholders Who Should Approve

- How close to what actually happens on the job is this?
- What parts do you think might be too easy or too difficult?
- What do you think of the way we will score the scenario?
- What would you recommend we do to improve this?

Critical Success Factors

To ensure your success in this task,

get these right and you are well on our way.

Factor	What You Need to Do
1. Realism	✓ **Make the scenario, challenges presented, decision choices, and the consequences of those choices (feedback) as realistic as possible.** The more realistic, the greater transfer to the job.
2. Sounding board	✓ **Have someone to bounce ideas off of, to work with during design** who can go through the scenario with you over and over again, brainstorm with you
3. Level of detail	✓ **Keep to a moderate level of detail in this task.** Spending large amounts of time on detail like all the questions or the script for a video at this stage runs a strong risk of being wasted because many things change as the scenario evolves.

Task 4: Build a Prototype

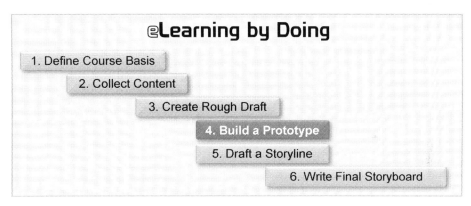

Why do we need a prototype? If you don't already have one or are not thoroughly familiar with what you can and cannot do in the authoring tool, now is the time to find out. In addition, it will give your stakeholders a much better idea of what you are trying to do. It is a whole lot better to get them on board now, get their ideas, and find out what they want to change on a small scale rather than have it all done just to find out they don't like this or that.

What's Going on Here?

If your organization does *not* already have a standard e-learning template, then see Task 2 in my earlier book, *Designing Effective eLearning*. You may want to review that information anyway as much of it applies to scenario-based courses regarding the technical design of an e-learning course.

If it does have a standard template, you still need to build a prototype because frequently scenario-based courses call for changes in the way things are done.

Both screen layout and navigation are more important in scenario-based courses than in linear courses. One reason is that you are striving for a greater real-world experience – the more you can make it look it look like the real world, the more the learner will become engaged in the scenario and the more they will take back to the workplace.

Another reason is that content delivery in a scenario is frequently not linear. All information sources will not be readily available or pushed at the learner like they are in the typical e-learning course. Learners may have to hunt around for them from time to time. Making sure the learner knows how to move around and how to get information will be critical.

Your prototype should have sample pages for each section of the course including samples of each type of scenario page.

- Opening pages
- Content pages
- Scenario pages
- Wrap-up pages
- Support pages

Key Point 6: Remember you goal with a prototype is to make sure everything is going to work as planned and your stakeholders approve the design.

That being the case,

- These pages to not have to have the final graphics, just something to give a pretty good idea of what you have in mind;

- The scenario interactive pages should work and the overall results/scoring.

Steps in This Task

Step	Deliverables
1. Create the screen layout(s)	Samples of different page layouts you plan to use
2. Create typical pages	Sample of each typical page
3. Review with stakeholders	Approved prototype

Step 1: Create the Screen Layout

As you start to think about your course layout, you will quickly realize that you will have several broad types of pages: the standard looking opening pages and content pages and the scenario pages. *They do not have to look the same!*

I am going to assume you have some kind of standard template for the standard pages. What is covered here focuses on the scenario pages.

Background that Represents the Environment/Setting

See if you can find some kind of a background or picture that will represent the workplace. If you plan to put graphics on top of it, be sure you have addressed transparency issues before getting too far along. Here are a few obvious examples:

- A faded picture of the workplace (store interior, office, production plant, customer service desk as seen by a customer service agent not a customer i.e. from the back, not the front) as the background (be careful that the learner can still read the text)
- A smaller picture of the same but instead of being a background, sits to the side.

- A picture of the scaffold in a safety course where the hazards were located
- A picture of parts of the service desk

When possible, have pictures of the objects that are part of the scene. Worst case, at least have clipart of the things you are talking about.

You can provide the learner with additional information about the characters or additional resources when they click or mouse over the character's picture or some kind of icon.

Navigation

You really do have a lot of choices about how you the learner navigates. We have mentioned a few already in previous chapters but let's recap and add more ideas.

Next button

This is probably the most common button in e-learning as far as I can tell. I know this may sound like heresy but consider alternatives. You will find that many times the Next button is not needed because decisions are being made.

- How about "Continue" (with the scenario) as it keeps one in the scenario a bit more than "Next"?
- No Next button at all (maybe you need a stiff drink about now) and the learner clicks on buttons that take them to one of three choices.
- Drag and drop one object to somewhere and you take them there in the course (Drag the employee (kicking and screaming) into your office.)
- Click some place on a geographic map or map of the plant.
- Click on an area on a conveyor belt and you take them to the page that examines it more closely.
- Click on the employee you want to work with next.

With respect to using arrows instead of text, I have seen no research on the matter. The only point would be that if your course will be crossing cultures, arrows are more universal.

And finally, in some scenarios, there is no next page. You do everything on one page like running diagnostic tests by clicking on different diagnostic machines.

Back and Previous buttons

The next most common button is a Back button – the one that takes you back to the previous page you were on. Some systems make a distinction between Back, which works like the internet browser Back button, and Previous, which takes you the numerically lower page in the course. In scenarios, there is little need for the Previous button unless you are using it in some book-like reference material (where your content is) such as the Manager's Guide.

Whether or not you even have a Back button is up for grabs. Since one of the underlying foundations of a scenario is a timeline, which it moves forward in time, having a Back button does not really fit as we do not yet have a time machine. Most games and simulations do not have one. If you must, maybe you can make it available for the lowest level learner as part of the learner customization.

Home button

In a scenario, where is home? Command central? The main office? Use home for something like that instead of taking you back to the beginning of the scenario. And, of course, if you do that, change the name to "Main office", "Customer Service Desk", etc.

Exit button

No comment here. Probably need to have one.

Help button

While I use Help buttons myself, I restrict the help to navigation help and other information about how to move around. I try refrain from things like Glossaries, References, etc. when possible. Make these available naturally within the scenario using things like corporate library, policy manual, SME notes …

Because scenarios can get quite complicated, a standard obvious way of navigating should be used. Navigation help should always be just one click away to answer questions like:

- "Ok, what am I supposed to do on this page?"
- "I made my choice, now what?"
- "What are my resources"

Location of Navigation

First, there is no hard and fast rule about where things should be. Some research indicates that the learner tends to scan the screen in the same direction as the culture they come from reads. Based on this, many people insist on putting the navigation buttons in the lower right but that is not necessary. Most people who are taking e-learning courses have had some exposure to the internet and are likely familiar with toolbars and web pages. They know to look along the top for controls. So, you can put your controls along the top or at the bottom for the repeated ones. Consistency is important – don't move them around unless it is necessary. (If you keep moving them around, the learner spends part of their effort looking for controls which has nothing to do with what you want them to learn or be able to do.)

Page numbers

Page numbers when covering *content* are fine. However, page numbers in a scenario are not. These can detract from the scenario experience. We don't have page numbers in our working environment. Page numbers tell learners how far along they are. And likewise, in the work environment, we have other things that tell us how far along we are and maybe how far we have to go.

- We have clocks and calendars which you might be able to use instead.
- If you are teaching a procedure or process, maybe there is some indication of the process step or stage.
- If you are moving through a physical landscape, the scenery changes.
- And sometimes we just do *not* know how far along we are like
  - when we are diagnosing a problem – you make guesses at the cause and then try something to see if that cause is the correct one.

- when we are trying to convince someone of something – we have to read body language and other non-verbal signals to tell whether or not they are convinced.

Also, in a branching scenario, the page number can be misleading because not all pages are being shown and you may be revisiting the same page.

Step 2: Create Typical Pages

 Best Practice 14: Once you have your typical background and navigation, create typical pages for each scenario section to give your reviewers a good feel for what the course will look like.

Build Sample pages

A Few Opening Pages

These should be easy. Just copy them from an existing course and tweak. For now, simply put a placeholder page for the scenario description.

A Little Content

This should be similar to your existing linear courses. Just put a sample page or two here.

Scenario Opening Instructions

Take a brief stab at what you think the instructions might be. Note to the reader that this will be finalized later.

Scenario Opening Learner customization

What is important is to create and pilot whatever learner customization options you are going to use. Make sure you can do in the authoring tool what you proposed in the rough draft. You will also be making sure it is learner friendly.

Scenario Interaction Segments

Guideline 13: Creating sample interactions is *the* most important part of the prototype. Using the list of typical interactions you created in the previous task, create a working prototype of each type of interaction including feedback and scoring.

For each one you will have some kind of situation descriptors, learner decision options, and interaction behavior that includes feedback and scoring.

Situation Descriptors

Create at least one interaction using each kind of situation descriptor you have decided to use.

- Text
- Pictures, diagrams, maps
- Audio
- Video
- Animation
- Meters/gauges

Learner Decision Options

Create at least one interaction for each method the learners would use to indicate their decisions.

- Multiple choice or multiple response
- Drag and drop
- Fill-in-the-blank
- Dropdown lists
- Hotspots on a map, picture, or diagram
- Ranking
- Matching
- Menus
- Slider bars
- Clicking on buttons

- Click on an object

Interaction Behavior Considerations

You need to demonstrate for the reviewers:

- When feedback is given (immediately, other)
- How feedback is given
- How the learner will access support resources
- How you will tell the learner which selections are not so good and which are better (shading, color codes, symbols like checks and Xs)
- Limiting the number of tries
- How you will make the interaction required (How will you prevent learners from going to the next page until they have made a choice? How will they know what is preventing them from moving forward?)
- How you will record their choice for later scoring

Best Practice 15: Make sure your prototype works under all conditions, not just the first time interactions are encountered.

- The first attempt is correct
- When the first and all subsequent attempts are incorrect
- The learner returns during the same session (How do you want it to work? Show the previous answer? What if that was wrong?)
- The learner closes out in the middle and returns the next day?

You may also need to test whether or not your design is 508 compliant.

Scenario Results and Debrief

In this section, display how the learner performed in the scenario. You may need to show various statistics like counts of correct, almost correct, etc. You may need to display different text and graphics depending on how learners scored. This should all be working in the prototype using the sample interactions you created.

In addition to how they did, you may need to help them debrief – help them figure out why they did poorly and what they need to do to improve. Now is the time to be sure the design you came up with in the Rough draft will work.

Wrap-up

There is nothing special here. Just put a few placeholder pages.

Support

As in the previous sections, you should have an example of each type of support that you plan to make available to learners.

Step 3: **Review with Stakeholders**

This is critical! Once you have done your own review, review your prototype with your stakeholders including target audience (e-learners). If they have any significant suggestions or issues, update the prototype and repeat the review.

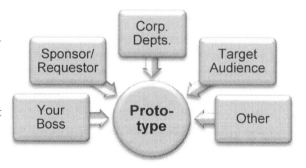

Stakeholders Who Approve the Prototype

Critical Success Factors

To ensure your success in this task,

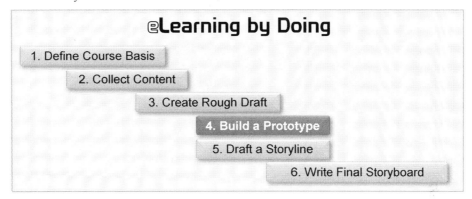

get these right and you are well on our way.

Factor	What You Need to Do
1. Sample of all key pages	✓ **Create a sample of all the key pages** to ensure that the design will work and stakeholders approve.
2. Working interactions and scoring	✓ **Create an example of each kind of interaction to be sure that it will work in authoring tool and that the stakeholders approve.** This is critical to your scenario. The whole purpose of your prototype is to ensure that you can create the proposed interactions and show the proper scoring.

Task 5: Draft a Storyline If Needed

What's Going on Here?

Some scenarios such as coaching, supervision, and sales may call for a storyline that describes the events. If yours does, then this chapter is for you. If not, just jump to writing the final story board.

Task 5: Draft a Storyline If Needed

While this is really part of the next task, it is so big that it needs its own chapter. Also, if you have a team working on this, writing a story takes a special talent and you may have another team member do this part.

The following may seem a bit mechanical and it will likely not produce a blockbuster movie, but you have a deadline to meet for this course. Let's get started!

I have used all three of these ways to lay out the scenario. Each has advantages.

- Use 3x5 cards or 1/2 sheets of paper on a table or taped to a wall
- MS Word®
- PowerPoint®

If you are doing this with other people, I suggest the first one and a large conference table or the third one using PowerPoint®. In the third one you find a conference room with a blank wall. Get a computer and a printer. Outline the story as best you can making notes on the PPT slides. Print them and tape to the wall. Everyone looks at it and makes suggestions. As they are made, the computer person makes the change in PPT and prints the changed pages and replaces on the wall. Some organizations have large projectors where you can use PowerPoint® sections and the slide sorter view. (See your PowerPoint® guru for more on these features.)

Other than that, you just have to try and see which one works for you.

Steps in This Task

While working at any one step in this task, you may find you have to go back to a previous step and make changes. If you are unfamiliar with writing scenarios or stories, this will give you a place to start and some good pointers.

Step		Deliverables
1.	Envision a "story-world"	Description of the story-world
2.	Start with the tried and true Hollywood formula	None

Step	Deliverables
3. Review/refine the scenario situation and goal	Refined situation description and goal
4. Identify obstacles/problems	List of obstacles/problems to be used as a basis for the interactions/questions
5. Write character descriptions	Character descriptions
6. Write the story	Story
7. Remove the boring bits	Better story
8. Review with stakeholders	Approved story – not necessarily better!

Step 1: Envision a "Story-*world*", Not a Story

Chris Crawford is a strong advocate of this (albeit for different reasons). Think about the environment where the action will take place. Make some notes about who is there, how things work, internal politics, what might be at risk, etc. Why? A scenario is generally linear – goes along a single path and timeline. If you are going to allow the learner to make decisions, then there are several paths, hopefully many, which the learner can follow. By thinking about the "scenario-world" you can much more easily build many different paths or sets of choices. If you think about a scenario, you automatically limit yourself to a single set of choices.

Tips for Coming Up with Story-worlds:

Technique 8: How to come up with a story-world:

1. Do *not* begin with your learning objectives or the content. For now, they *can* easily get in the way. But don't panic. These will come back into play in just a little while. Why? Because right now you need to focus on an interesting scenario, not what is to be learned.

2. Brainstorm any ideas you have for a scenario first. You only get one chance to approach this with an empty mind. Use it well.

3. Now review the war stories you heard while collecting data.
   - What problems were solved?
   - What things went wrong?
   - What obstacles had to be overcome?
   - What challenges did they face?

4. How can you turn these into some kind of a mystery or interesting challenge for the learner?

5. If you don't have any good ideas yet, go back to the SMEs and new hires and ask for more war stories.

Tips About Stories:

Tip 13: Remember that one story or scenario is not always sufficient. You may need multiple scenarios:

- To cover all material.
- To gradually get more challenging – if you make it too hard or easy, they will bail out.
- To make it interesting and allow the learner to make significant decisions.

So, come up with several ideas. It is a lot easier to throw them away than make them up later. Also, you may find that you can combine them into an even better scenario story.

Tip 14: As you introduce more difficult tasks in the later scenarios, keep some easy bits to:

- Maintain interest

- Repeat important material
- Keep confidence up

Tip 15: Don't be afraid to use a bit of humor.

Tip 16: Know in advance that you will be going back to get more data.

Tip 17: A story and the development of its characters are far more important than graphics.

Step 2: Use the Tried and True Hollywood Formula

"One very clear definition of a good story requires that it have a hero who has a goal but who must face an obstacle standing in the way of reaching that goal. The bigger the obstacle, the better the story." (Iuppa & Borst, 2007, p. 39)

The Formula

The Hollywood approach is to have a hero/heroine trying to attain a goal but that is not a story. There must be something that *gets in the way* of attaining the goal – some obstacles. The interest in the story (plot) comes as the main character overcomes the obstacles (problems, complications) and achieves the goal.

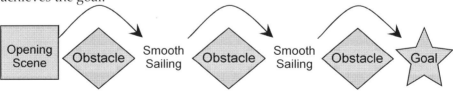

Learn from the Experts

Watch a couple of mysteries, detective shows, or action movies with this formula in mind. You will most likely see it and it will be easier for you write a story. Then think about the situation the main character faced. What was the goal? What were the obstacles he/she had to overcome?

Now the secret! Create at least one obstacle for each task/skill/sub-skill. This way you will be sure that the learner will exit the course being able to perform the performance goals/objectives for the course. Having two or more obstacles would be better.

The Problem with the Formula

It is linear and is designed for stories that follow along only one path. The formula is not designed to be interactive. To make your scenario interesting you will need to allow the learner to make meaningful decisions and possibly follow different paths through the storyline. Be careful this does not get too complicated. Remember your overall goal is for *them* to *master the material and apply it on the job.*

Step 3: Review/Refine the Scenario Situation and Goal

Situation: You have a rough idea what this is based on your rough draft. You may want to refine it just a bit here to make sure it still fits with the kinds of interactions you now have in mind.

Goal: You should already have this from your earlier work. This was also covered a little earlier when we talked about the challenge. If you do not, then do it now. Remember, this is the *scenario* goal, *not* the *course* purpose.

- Sell someone a phone
- Handle a customer complaint
- Diagnose a car/patient/machine/computer problem
- Increase production in your unit
- Go a week without an accident
- Find and put out a ___ fire
- Assess/evaluate ___

Step 4: Identify Obstacles/Problems for Interactions

Here is where you tie the scenario to the performance objectives and content. You develop obstacles such that, in order to overcome them, the learner has to use the information provided and/or demonstrate the skills needed (at least as best as we can do electronically.) These will provide the foundation for the exercises.

Guideline 14: Come up with more interactions (questions) than you need because you will likely throw some out later.

Guideline 15: Put these between the situation described in the opening scene and the goal.

Ex: Scaffolding Safety Course

> Hazards that are evident as one approaches the scaffolding
> Hazards as one climbs up or down the scaffolding
> Hazards one could encounter as one works on top of the scaffolding

Ex: Coaching Course

> Team member 1 has low skills.
> Team member 2 has low skills and low motivation.
> Team member 3 has low skills and average motivation.
> Team member four has average motivation and average skills.

Guideline 16: Now review the obstacles to be sure that if the learner overcomes the obstacles, they will the learning content be covered and getting closer to the goal.

Step 5: Write Character Descriptions

Most likely you will need a brief description of each character.

Note that characters may change as the scenario progresses. For example, if you are coaching them, they may improve, stay the same, or get worse in skill or motivation level.

Ex: Scaffolding Safety Course

> You are new to the job and have no experience working around scaffolding. It all seems easy enough but you cannot figure out why you are having so much trouble. You try hard but still keep making mistakes.

Ex: Coaching Course

> Sam is the lowest performing member of the team. He is a likable guy and seems motivated. The word is he does not have the skills.
>
> Greta seems to always have low motivation. Like Sam, her performance is low. The difference is that Greta has been on your team for nearly a year and seems to be able to do everything fairly well. You have asked questions to determine the cause and the best you can figure now is that she is not very motivated.

Step 6: **Write the Story**

A story is broken down into scenes. Each scene may have one or more obstacles to overcome. Think about a car chase scene in a movie. They are speeding down the highway. Suddenly someone is crossing the road. Next a truck pulls out. Then the hero turns the wrong way down a one-way street. He zips around a tanker truck and one of the bad guys slams into it. But two are still on his tail. His partner shoots a tire out of the second chase car. Still one more to go. …

You get the idea. Each scene can have several interactions to make a point related to the content.

Technique 9: **How to create a storyline using the Hollywood formula:**

1. Start with your setting.
2. Jot the essence of each war story on a 3x5 card.
   - Situation
   - Problem (which will lead to one or more interactions in your scenario)

- How the problem was solved (which will lead to choices)
3. Arrange them in some kind of logical flow on a large table.
4. Add bits to make it more interesting and smooth out the flow.

Step 7: **Remove the Boring Bits → Make It Fun**

"The worst simulation games are merely a set of learning points with the simulation part designed only as a sneaky way to get the player to each of them. The best keep pulling you to continue to the end in spite of yourself." (Prensky, 2007, p. 215)

Guideline 17: Focus on challenge while remembering that not everyone likes competition.

- Any one of a number of scenario types can work:
  - Mystery / detective
  - Action / adventure
- Personalize the goal
- Get better. While watching shows, ask yourself what makes this movie/show interesting? Make notes.

What makes the goal work is the story (context (environment & situation)) wrapped around it.

Chris Crawford says to focus on paring away the boring decisions. Make sure the decisions you have the learner make truly have an impact on the scenario and are *not* obvious or trivial. Don't underestimate your learner's ability to figure things out. If in doubt, create a pilot on paper and try it out. Get some feedback.

And one more time, don't be afraid to use a bit of humor.

Step 8: **Review with Stakeholders**

Like all the previous steps, it is best to get this approved before going too far. Here it is unlikely that you will need all of them. The key ones are shown here. You may want to simply run a list of the obstacles/interactions by a few SMEs.

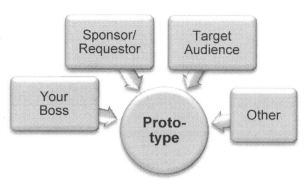

Stakeholders Who Approve the Story

Critical Success Factors

Other than having a story wizard on your team, here are some of the critical success factors that will help you write a better story-line.

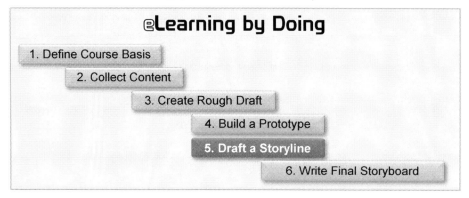

Factor	What You Need to Do
1. Number of story writers	✓ **Get a partner.** Single person designs are considerable *less* effective that two person designs.
2. Focus	✓ Avoid getting too caught up in delivering the content while you write the scenario. There will be plenty of time for that later.
3. Realism	✓ **Maintain the real flavor of the work environment** to ensure transfer back to the workplace.

Task 6: Write the Final Storyboard

Why a Storyboard?

Better instructional design
The main reason to spend the time writing a storyboard is to focus on the *instructional* design. In most cases, putting the course content directly into an authoring tool can get you sidetracked with the technical details of the authoring

tool. Trying to do both at the same time frequently results in poorly designed course. In general, a well-designed course takes about two to three times as much time to *design* as it does to *develop* in an authoring tool.

Better reviews

A second reason for a storyboard is that usually reviewers can make changes and suggestions in the storyboard easier than they can in the authoring software (Lectora®, Articulate®, Toolbook®, Captivate®, Authorware®, etc.). In fact, most reviewers do not even have the authoring tool. You want their input. If it is hard for them to do, then you are going to get less than their best.

A third reason is that a storyboard should show all the hidden objects, text, and feedback to questions. It may be hard for the reviewer to view *all* the feedback if it is in an authoring tool.

Save time

A fourth reason is that it is usually easier to put an approximation of the course into a storyboard *describing* how it will behave compared to actually spending many hours actually *developing* it. For example, you may be able to *describe* an exercise in five minutes compared to 30-60 minutes *developing* it and making it work. It is better to spend just 5 minutes and have it changed than 30 minutes and have it changed or discarded. The same holds true for any audio or video. Redoing these can eat up a lot of time and money.

What's Going on Here?

By now, you should have everything you need to complete your course design.

- ✓ Course purpose
- ✓ Audience description
- ✓ Stakeholders
- ✓ Performance objectives

✓ Content
✓ Rough draft
✓ Working prototype
✓ Storyline if needed

In this task, you pull all this together and write the course content and the scenario in the form of a storyboard. Let's look again at a detailed view of the course sections.

Sections of a Scenario Course

Section	Contents/Components	
1. Opening Pages	<ul><li>Welcome</li><li>Introduction</li><li>Qualification questions (optional)</li><li>Benefits and/or negative case study</li><li>Expectations (objectives)</li><li>Explanation of the course approach</li></ul>	
2. Content	Abbreviated content as some can be delivered within the scenario, frequently *presented as a briefing*	
3. Scenario	Opening	<ul><li>Restate the scenario challenge</li><li>Interface/ Navigation Instructions page(s)</li><li>Learner customization page(s) if any</li></ul>
	Interaction Segments	<ul><li>Interactions where learners make decisions (usually questions but not always) and get feedback</li></ul>
	Results	<ul><li>Summary of how they did with as much analysis as possible</li><li>Debriefing</li></ul>
4. Wrap-up	<ul><li>Summary of what was covered, important points to remember</li><li>Next steps</li></ul>	
5. Support	Popup pages containing any kind of support material used by learners	

Steps in This Task

Here are the steps. The deliverables from each step are obvious.

Step
1. Select your storyboarding tool
2. Write your course opening section
3. Write your content section
4. Write your scenario opening pages
5. Write the scenario interactions
6. Finalize the results section
7. Write the wrap-up section
8. Write the support section
9. Finish up

A Word about Consistency

Before we get started, I want to say just one thing about being consistent, especially within the scenario.

Guideline 18: Be consistent about how the learner interacts with the scenario. The more variety, the more the learner focuses on the technology and *not* on the scenario or the content.

This is especially true if you have several people working on the scenario. Make all the interactions work the same, use the same kind of buttons, and deliver the same kind of feedback in the same way.

Step 1: Select Your Storyboarding Tool

At this point in the process, your scenario is either on pieces of paper or maybe in a word processor. This is a good time to convert it to a format that can be understood and reviewed by your stakeholders – the SMEs, your boss, the sponsors, etc.

I typically use PowerPoint®. I do *not* use any formal storyboard layout because I have found that layouts with lots of boxes take a long time to complete and add little to the final design. I take this simple approach.

Technique 10: Effective use of a storyboard:

1. Take a snapshot of a blank screen from the prototype and put that in the background in the storyboard (on the master slide in PowerPoint®).
2. Use fonts and font sizes the same as I would in the target course.
3. Put notes *about* what is to happen on the screen either in yellow text blocks or in the Notes area in PowerPoint®.
4. When the reviewers make comments, have them either use PowerPoint® notes or yellow text blocks on the screen. I rarely use PowerPoint® comments because it takes extra effort to read them. You can't do something to show them all easily like you can in MS Word®.
5. If reviewers want to change the text, they use the line-through style (~~abc~~) to delete text and new text in red.

Step 2: Write Your Course Opening Section

It is time to develop the content that is to appear on those pages.

- Welcome/splash
- Course introduction
- Qualification questions (optional)
- Expectations (Objectives)
- Benefits and/or negative case study
- Set the stage

Welcome Page

This page welcomes learners to the course. It provides them with enough information to be sure they are in the right course. It sets the tone for the course. Here is one place where it is worth spending some hours on good graphics.

If you have a poorly done welcome page, it will detract from the rest of the course. It does *not* have to be flashy or very fancy, just professional. It should be at roughly the same level as the rest of the course.

Guideline 19: Make your course fit the culture of the work environment and the topic. If it is a serious topic, have a serious looking welcome page; if it is a casual topic or a casual work environment, give your welcome page a casual look.

Guideline 20: Keep this page relatively clean and make it dramatic. Use a minimum of text and some powerful relevant graphics if you have the budget for them.

Here are some of the typical items you can include on this page:

- Fancy graphic
- Learner's name
- Course title
- Revision Number
- Published Date
- Copyright

Course Introduction Page

This page further orients learners to the course. There is no particular order for these items and sometimes people include one or more of these on the Welcome page. Just don't get the Welcome page too cluttered.

Components of Introduction Page

Component	Example
1. Brief description	Ex: "This course explains some techniques to help you supervise employees with differing skill and motivation levels."
2. Whom the course was designed for	Ex: "This course is designed for first level managers (supervisors) who are candidates for the advanced management training program." In a way, this, in combination with the brief course description, describe the *setting* where the content of the course will be applied or used.
3. The purpose of the course	Ex: "The purpose of this course is to increase productivity by improving your coaching skills." **This links the course to business outcomes.** It describes their role within the setting i.e. how they are going to use this information. Sometimes this can appear on the Benefits page.
4. Prerequisites	Ex: "You should already have taken Supervision I."
5. Estimated time to complete	Ex: "Estimated Time to Complete: 1/2 Hour"
6. Assessment	Ex: "After completing this course, you will take an exam. You must pass that exam with a score of at least 90% to qualify for the advanced management training program."

Component	Example
7. How to navigate button	If you don't have the "How to Navigate" page in line, then you need a button that opens up a window that describes how to move around within the course.
8. Audio note	If it is not obvious, inform learners if you are using audio. Tell them how to turn it on, pause it and resume, replay it, and turn it off. If you have closed caption text available for hearing impaired, tell them how to show and hide that text.
9. Where to get additional help	Ex: "If you have questions on this material or feel you need additional help, contact ___."

Qualification Questions Page (optional)

If there are some prerequisites for this course or some knowledge, skills, or experience you need the learner to have before starting this course, ask questions now. Let them know if this course is not appropriate for them.

If you don't already, you might want to have a few questions at the beginning of your course to be sure that the learner is not in over their head. Not a pretest as such, but a few questions to be sure the material is appropriate for them.

Ex: "Have you been supervising for at least 2 months? If so, click here to continue. If not, please click Exit and contact your manager."

Ex: "Have you ever sold any ___ products? …"

Ex: "Have you taken the advanced course in ___?"

Benefits or Negative Case Study Page

While the need for most courses is obvious, what does it hurt to increase motivation a little? Some people may not be aware of all of the benefits or of the negative consequences if the content is not applied.

Key Point 7: The benefits page is key to motivating the learner. If the value of this course is not obvious, you should make a strong case for taking it. **If you can't write a good benefits page, you may have a stupid course on your hands.**

Answer the question, "Why should I take this course?" or "What's in it for me?" Here is where you make the course relevant to the learner. Adult learners want to see clearly its practical uses, especially how it can help them do specific tasks, avoid problems, or be more successful on the job.

You can go with listing the benefits or a negative case study which describes some bad news consequences when the content was not applied.

Benefits

Best Practice 16: List as many personal benefits to the learner as possible.

Include:

✓ Expected benefits to learner

✓ Expected benefits to the organization (some version of the course purpose which includes the business need and how this training addresses that need)

✓ Negative consequences if the training is not successful

Tip 18: You can just state the benefits or you can use:

- Testimonials
- Hard data or statistics
- Stories of things going right or wrong
- A dramatic demonstration
- A video of things going right
- A description of a challenge they might be facing – one where this course will help them meet that challenge and come out a winner
  - Create tension by describing where they are now and where they would like to be or could end up.

- Is this your situation? ... Wouldn't you like to be able to ...?
- Our company is facing ... Wouldn't you like to move from being part of the problem to part of the solution?

Negative Case Study

You can include a page that describes a situation similar to your scenario that ended up with negative consequences. This can be useful to set the stage for your scenario. You might end it with something like:

"Would you want this to happen to you?"

"Would you know how to avoid this?"

"Would you know how to handle situations like this?"

Expectations (Objectives)

This is a list of what the learner will be expected to do at the end of the course. They are framed as challenging expectations instead of boring objectives. "After completing this course, you will be *expected* to be able to ..." For more details on converting objectives to expectations, see *Designing Effective eLearning*.

Set-the-Stage Page

Best Practice 17: Set the stage for the content and briefly introduce the scenario. If you can, make it tie in somehow with the negative case study given earlier.

You can put this as the last page of your Introduction section or the first page of the Content, wherever it fits best.

Ex: "First you will get a briefing on ___. Then you will have a chance to apply what you learned. You will be in charge of ___. Production is having some real problems ... (situation). Your job is to see if you can ___."

Ex: "A new model of our top selling cell phone has just come out. As you start your day, you will be given a briefing on the new phone. Then your goal is to sell a phone to at least one customer before the day is over. Let's get started by clicking the **Briefing** button below."

Ex: "You have just been promoted to supervisor. You begin your first day by attending a briefing on supervision principles. Then you will go to work. You have inherited a team that has some problems. Your goal is to get the team back on track and production up to the company standard. Click the **Briefing** button to get started."

When you use this kind of lead-in for the content, the learner will start off with a good solid reason to learn the material and as a result will be more likely to:

- Pay closer attention
- Make an effort to understand and retain the information
- Apply it back on the job

Step 3: Write Your Content Section

Decide How Will You Present Content

Remember Gee's "Human beings are quite poor at using verbal information when given lots of it out of context and before they can see how it applies to actual situations. They use verbal information **best** [emphasis added] when it is given "just in time" (when they can put it to use) and "on demand" (when they feel they need it)." (Gee 2007 p. 37) I mentioned at the beginning? Well here is where it begins to come into play.

In standard linear courses, you just tell them what you needed to tell them. Well, now you have to embed it some way so that it becomes part of the scenario. This usually is *not* too difficult.

Here are just a few of many ideas to imbed content:

- Salesperson's Memory Jogger by clicking on an icon for it
- Supervisor's Pocket Guide by clicking on an icon for it
- FAQs
- Diagrams – click on an icon to bring the diagram up, then click on part of the diagram for more info
- Asking questions of the customer/employee or a more experienced person, your boss

- Click on a phone to ask an expert.
- Drag a picture of the main character into the boss's office to ask a question.
- Checking in a file cabinet(s) for info
- Freedom to ask questions somehow
- Multiple paths not shown in original scenario. i.e. scenario now needs to be more flexible than the original one
- And of course, a briefing before the scenario starts

Write Your Content

See *Designing Effective eLearning* for extensive coverage of how to design this part of your course. If you have *not* had formal training in how to write web-based training, then do yourself and your learners a favor and get that book. For a very small price you will greatly improve the effectiveness of your courses.

For now, here is that book in a nutshell:

Technique 11: How to write the content section – short version:

1. Organize your content into logical chunks and apply one of the classic organization types to presenting the material so it will be understood and remembered.
2. Write an overview of the entire content letting the learner know what is coming and how it is organized.
3. Introduce each chunk/topic with an overview.
4. Have an applied exercise or two every 5 pages or so.
5. End each chunk/topic with a summary that is something like a job aid, not a list of topics or objectives.
6. End the entire with a summary of the important points for the entire content.

Guideline 21: Keep the tone and language in keeping with a briefing or within the context of the scenario for greatest effect. Talk directly to the learner as though the boss was giving the briefing.

Using Video in Your Content

> *"The reason people try to do things that might not be the most productive way, is because they think they can do it better, and even if they have been told that such a way doesn't work, they haven't been clearly informed on the overall outcome until after their incorrect actions are already completed.* Cliff Perry, personal email, 2013.

In some cases, you can easily record a video of what happens when you do it wrong and how to do it right. This is easily done with today's smart phones that can record HD video.

Step 4: Write Your Scenario Opening Pages

As you launch into your scenario, there are several pages you write that get the learner off to a good start.

> *"Make scenarios easy enough to understand, so that when a person enters into them, they aren't frazzled wondering if they will get it wrong or right, let them learn from both. Show them what happens in both. Sometimes people blindly guess for the right answers, get them right, and never actually learn what it is they were supposed to have knowledge of in the first place. You want people to learn from the people who have succeeded as well as those who have not.* (Cliff Perry, personal email, 2013.)

> *"I have not failed. I've just found 10,000 ways that won't work."*
>
> — Thomas A. Edison

> *"I didn't fail the test, I just found 100 ways to do it wrong."*
>
> — Benjamin Franklin

Technique 12: How to write effective opening pages for the scenario:

1. Write the scenario description including the challenge.
2. Write the interface instructions (if needed)
3. Design and write the learner customization page.

Scenario Description Page (Introduction)

This page is critical! It provides motivation for learners to pay attention to the upcoming content.

Best Practice 18: If you can, use their name on this page. If you do, use it like it would be used on the job. Sometimes this is the last name instead of the first.

Clarify as needed any part of the setting, environment, characters, or situation needed. Decide on the role of the learner. Will they be the main character? In some cases this may be too risky for the learner. If you think it might be, you can place them in the role of an advisor to main character – "What would advise the supervisor to do now?" (This is better than "What do you think the supervisor should do now?" because it keeps the learner in the scenario.)

Here is where you fully describe the situation for the scenario. Include only information needed to complete the scenario. This might be a good time for a short video – *no more than* 2 minutes.

Try to end with a challenge to the learner that is job related. Here are few examples.

- Ex: "Your job is to sell a phone to at least one customer before the day is over."
- Ex: "Your goal is to beat all the other teams out by processing over 100 claims this month and win the 2-day team vacation package."
- Ex: "Your goal is to get to the end of the week with no accidents or safety violations."
- Ex: "How many days can you go without an accident?"
- Ex: "Your job is to complete the tax form without errors."
- Ex: "See if you supervise so well that you get a promotion."
- Ex: "You have an employee that is producing (selling, ___) at only 50%. Your goal is to increase the employee's productivity (sales, ___) to 100%".
- Ex: "You have just been handed a pizza to deliver to a house 4 miles away. See if you can safely deliver it in less than 10 minutes."

Ex: "See how much you can sell/increase production/ ___."

Ex: "See how few defects you can let through."

Ex: Here is an excellent one from Allen (2007). Instead of *"Which of these meal tickets are added incorrectly?"*, he recommends something like *"In some months, Harry found his restaurant earned what he expected, but in others where he served the same meals and the same number of customers, he lost money and had to let staff go. Here are ___ typical meal checks from a month where he lost money. See if you can find Harry's problem."*

Write the Interface Instructions (if needed)

Some scenarios use standard navigation. If yours does, this is not needed. But, if you use a different way to navigate, let the learners know. This might be the case if you use a single page for performing diagnostics or any number of alternate navigation methods. Include:

- How to navigate
- What resources are available and how to access them
- What buttons or things can they click on to get help

Briefly describe anything they might want to know about how they will be scored or what they can and cannot do like move backward.

Write the Learner Customization Instructions (if needed)

When appropriate, have learners select an avatar and any other options you might have. We covered this back in Draft the Interface step (pg. 85) in the Create a Rough Draft task. Here is that short starter list again in case you forgot.

- Get their name if you haven't already
- Male/female pictures for the boss
- Male/female pictures for themselves
- Transcript on/off
- Sound on/off when it was not critical to the learning
- Different background pictures (one for an office and one for a store depending on where the sales person was located)

- Allowing the learner to select which of aspects of the multiple levels they want to include or exclude
- Allowing them to name to the characters
- Allowing them to specify their level of expertise which could control:
  - Question difficulty
  - Hints
  - Resources available
  - Whether or not they have a Back button

Step 5: Write the Scenario Interactions

Interactivity is *not* just clicking buttons or sliding things as we discussed earlier. You can open your car door and the interior lights go on. You did something and something happened. Some would call this interactivity but I wouldn't in the area of e-learning.

Best Practice 19: Make sure your interactions have the learner *apply* what they have learned.

Technique 13: How to write effective interactions for the scenario:

1. Before you write the final version of any interaction, finalize your scoring method.

2. Then outline your interactions and check against your performance objective.

3. Then for each interaction, write the:
   - Description - situation
   - Decision to be made(explanation, prediction, action, diagnostic, calculation, or coding question)
   - Realistic choices
   - Rich feedback including observable outcomes, hidden/delayed outcomes, instructional content, and a score

- Support available
- What happens next

Finalize Your Scoring Method If Any

Best Practice 20: Before you get into writing the details of the interactions, finalize your scoring method. It can make a big difference in how you write your interactions.

Decide how you will score the answers, compute the scenario score, and display it. Here is an example of scoring from a course about coaching an employee with low motivation. The numbers in [ ] show how his productivity changed.

"How would you coach Joe?"

- Give positive feedback very frequently (a couple of times a day). [+3]
- Give positive feedback once or twice a week. [0]
- Ask what is important to the agent about his job and what is missing. [+2]
- Schedule the agent for extra training courses. [-1]

Once you have this finalized, you will use it in every interaction so be reasonably sure you have the final version here.

Outline Your Interactions

Best Practice 21: Before you write all the details for each interaction, outline them all to make sure they flow well *and* that all your objectives are covered. Once you start writing the interaction, you can easily get lost in the details and forget some important questions to ask.

> *"Writing good questions can easily be the most time-consuming part of building your content [scenario]. (Ineffective questions can be written very quickly!) To make sure you stay on track, be sure to review your objectives carefully and always use them as your guide."* (Ward & Elkins, 2009. p. 129)

So begin with this list. Remember that your criteria is, "If learners make all the correct decisions (answer all the questions reasonably well), how sure am I that they have satisfied the objective?"

Technique 14: How to be sure all your performance objectives are covered:

This is one technique I have used successfully on many occasions. It is simple and quick to use. It has kept me from having too few questions for one objective and too many for another.

1. Take a Word® table or a spreadsheet and list the interactions down the left column as briefly as possible in the sequence they will appear to the learner.
2. Check the flow (transition from one to the next) to be sure they make sense in the real world.
3. Then, across the top of columns to the right, list your *performance* objectives.
4. For each interaction, put an X in the objective column it applies to.

	Obj 1	Obj 2	Obj 3	Obj 4
Interaction question 1	X			
Interaction question 2		X		
Interaction question 3				
Interaction question 4				X
Interaction question 5			X	

Best Practice 22: Review our questions and objectives and ask yourself, "Will the questions for each objective ensure that the learner has achieved the objective?" (I.e. are these the right questions to be asking?)

Diagram If Needed

If you have decided to use branching, then now is the time to draw a diagram of your scenario. See the different designs we covered back in the Rough Draft chapter on page 79.

General Guidelines

Guideline 22: Allow for experimentation – allow the learner to try one solution and see what happens, learn from any mistakes, and then try again. No, not all learners will try again, but many will.

Guideline 23: Introduce additional content by providing things like icons they can click to get more information.

"Human beings are quite poor at using verbal information when given lots of it out of context and before they can see how it applies to actual situations. They use verbal information best [emphasis added] when it is given 'just in time' (when they can put it to use) and 'on demand' (when they feel they need it)." (Gee, 2007, p. 37)

Guideline 24: Scenario and character development are far more important than graphics. If you have limited budget, put the energy into the scenario description and go lighter on the graphics.

Recruit someone to help with this part. A second set of eyes and ideas will make a huge difference!

Complete an Interaction Form for Each Interaction

You can use the following form to organize and write each interaction. Each of the components is described in more detail following the form.

Interaction (Scene) Components Form

Component	Description
1. Description	Who, where, when, what's happening (surroundings, environment, setting, context)

Component	Description
2. Decision (Question)	Write the question, usually in the second person. "What would you do?" "What would you tell the customer? Your boss?" "What is likely to happen next?"
3. Choices	4. Rich Feedback
	Observable Outcomes / Hidden/delayed Outcomes / Relevant Content / Scoring
A. ...	
B. ...	
C. ...	
...	
5. Support Available	Manuals, guides, etc.
6. Next Scene	

Let's look at each of these components.

Interaction Component 1: The Description

This is a description of the situation in this part of the scenario (characters, event, minor crisis, result of a previous action). Make it describe a real-world setting where the content will be applied.

- Who (all characters if it is a role-play scenario or components if it is a system)
- When & where (environment)
- What happened/how (situation)

Ex: The customer asks, "Will this phone work in my basement?"

Interaction Component 2: The Decision (Question)

As you refine the question, consider using one of these classes of questions, each of which has a different purpose. Once the scenario is rolling, your first impulse is to write questions that have learners decide on an action like, "What would you do?" However, there are others. Use more than one class to give your scenario variety and keep it from being boring.

Decision Classes

Class	Description
1. Prediction	Purpose: To predict what is likely to happen next. These questions have the learner predict the effects, outcomes, or results of what has happened. In some scenarios like project planning or assessment, you can ask prediction questions like,
	Ex: "Your boss asks what is likely to happen if this trend continues. What would you tell him/her?"
	Ex: "What do you think the customer will do if you avoid his question?"
	Ex: From a project management course: "In a meeting (without your computer), your boss just told you that Design DB task is going to be 3 days late. She asks you what the impact on the overall project will be. Which of the following would be most accurate?"
	Ex: From a coaching course: "You observe the boss discipline a fellow worker in front of others on the shop floor. Which of the below are likely outcomes of that action?" (The following question might be one where you ask them what they would do.)

Class	Description
2. Explanation	Purpose: To explain *why* things happened. In some scenarios, like a diagnosis, you can ask questions that help the learner see cause and effect – why things happened. It is important to keep it in the scenario context by having them give the explanation to someone.
	Ex: From a project management course: "Your teammate asks, 'Why would the project would come in a week late?' What would you say?"
	Ex: "The boss asks you, 'Why did these new recruits get such low scores?' What would you say?"
3. Action Choice	Purpose: To select a course of action. "What would you do?"
	Ex: "A student walks into your office and asks to register for Biology 2001. How would you do this?"
	Ex: From a project management course: "In a meeting (without your computer), your boss just told you that Design DB task is going to be 3 days late. What should you do?"
	Ex: From a coaching course: "Your numbers are way down for the current week. Which of the three groups of supervision techniques should you use to get your whole group rolling?

Class	Description
4. Diagnosis	Purpose: To get more information. You can also have the learner ask for more information. This is really a version of selecting a course of action but with a significant twist. The learner makes an inquiry and gets information to make future decisions. There really is no right or wrong, just better information. Ex: "Your customer is in a hurry. You have time for just two questions. Which ones would you like to ask?" Ex: "Select a diagnostic test to run." While you could give them feedback on which ones are better, the real purpose of the feedback here would be more information. The feedback would be what the customer said or the information from the diagnostic test.
5. Calculation	Purpose: To calculate or code. Have them calculate something or provide the correct coding/rating. Ex: "Enter the account for this expense." Ex: "Using the 20% tip rule, what is the tip for this meal?"
6. Coding/ Rating	Learners are being trained in some terminology, coding, or rating scheme. The questions would give them a situation and ask for their response. Ex: "Enter your diagnosis code." Ex: "Given the insurance claim above, what would your diagnosis code be?" Ex: "How would you rate this deficiency?"

A couple of warnings:

Warning 9: Avoid recall questions as much as possible -- questions that cannot be put in context of the scenario.

× "What gas should be used to …?"

× "Which of the following are correct?"

× "The ABC regulation requires employers to ___"

These limit transfer to the job. The whole reason for your course is to get learners to *use* the content. Right? So make the questions "learning by doing" questions.

Warning 10: Do not make the questions too easy or ridiculous because your scenario will become less interesting to the learner. Do you like playing a game where you know all the answers?

Guideline 25: Stop thinking of questions you are going to ask the learner and think about the decisions they will make on the job.

Computer Question Types

Once you have the questions, you can decide on how they will be implemented in your authoring software. Use this table, shown earlier in the Rough Draft chapter, to select the appropriate question type.

Decision to Computer Question Type

Decision	Computer Question Type
1. Selecting from a list of choices (text or graphics) –	Multiple choice (selecting *one* choice from a list) or
	Multiple response (check all that apply)
2. Rating items along a scale	Drag and drop
	Multiple choice
	Ordinal rating
	Slider bar

Decision	Computer Question Type
3. Categorizing or classifying items	Drag and drop (best)
	Compound multiple-choice single answer (1 for each item like a survey)
4. Identifying areas to be tested	Hotspots on a map, picture, or diagram
	Click on an object
	Multiple-choice
	Static or dropdown list/menu
5. Arranging things in sequence such as process steps, along a timeline, or order of importance	Drag and drop
6. Teaching the correct placement of items such as furniture or equipment	Drag and drop
7. Labeling a diagram or map	Drag and drop
	Matching
	Several fill-in-the-blank questions with the entry boxes near the point on the diagram or map
	Several multiple choice questions using a dropdown lists
8. Estimating/calculating an amount	Fill-in-the-blank (best)
	Multiple-choice single answer
	Slider bar
9. Entering the right code	Fill-in-the-blank (best)
	Multiple-choice single answer

Warning 11: Avoid True/False questions as they are usually too simplistic for scenarios and rarely if ever does a work situation call for True or False decision as such.

Warning 12: Avoid matching except when labeling a diagram or something similar. If you are trying to sort things out, use a drag a drop. A bunch of crisscrossed lines is not memorable.

Interaction Component 3: The Choices

Once you have the situation description and the question you are going to ask, design your choices. Good answer choices are critical to a good scenario. In most cases, questions should have at least three choices, four is better. Avoid going over seven choices.

Key Point 8: Poor answer choices can ruin the best scenario question.

In his book "Chris Crawford on Interactive Storytelling" on page 40, Chris says that "Interactivity depends on the choices available to the user." He had it printed in huge letters so the reader would see that it was important.

Try to follow these guidelines when writing the choices you present the learner with:

Guideline 26: Keep the choices within the context of the scenario, not external type questions – more or less real world decisions that will need to be made.

One author said that they should be "authentic decisions about what to say or do."

Guideline 27: Make their answers matter.

Britt found that engagement is evident when an individual feels a sense of responsibility for, and commitment to, a performance domain, so that performance matters to the individual. Thomas Britt, (referenced in Kathleen Iverson's article on Engaging the E-Learner: Interaction is Not Education. e-magazine, Feb 2008).

Guideline 28: The choices should use shades of gray if possible. The world is not black and white for the most part. Give answer choices that are distinct but different shades of gray.

In the real-world, most situations have several solutions. Some are better than others. Create your answer choices that reflect the fact that not every situation is black and white with one correct answer and everything else is incorrect. When you do this, you should give feedback that matches the answer choice. Make the answers to the question cover a range of possibilities giving more points for better answers and fewer points for not so good answers. All you do is simply weigh the choices something like this.

Worst answer = 0 or even -1
Good answer = 1
Better answer = 2
Best = 3

Guideline 29: The choices should be a reasonable level of difficulty. Do not make them too hard because this will frustrate the learner.

Guideline 30: The choices should be straightforward. Avoid compound answer choices that use the word "and." Instead, break the answer choices apart and have the learner "Check all that apply."

Guideline 31: Present choices in a logical order. If the question has numeric choices, present them in numerical order (10, 20, 30, 40 not 20, 40, 30, 10).

Guideline 32: Make them similar length. People know that the longer answers are more likely to be correct.

Guideline 33: Make the answer choices parallel in construction (singular/plural, verb tense, a/an).

Guideline 34: Avoid "None of the above" or "All of the above". First of all, this is not very realistic and will draw learners out of the scenario. And, here are some more reasons.

<u>None of the above</u>

This implies that there is a correct answer that is not given. When this answer is the correct one, there is no way to determine if the student is thinking of the actual correct answer.

<u>All of the above</u>

When directed to select the "best" answer, then "all of the above" cannot logically be chosen. Also, learners in a hurry tend to read the first correct answer and stop. Instead, it is better to use a different type of question with directions like "Check all that apply." Another reason is that this is frequently the right answer so if someone is guessing, they are likely to pick it.

Make the Choices Natural When You Can

When dealing with spoken response choices like "What would you say?" you can make your choices exact quotes (natural) or simply state the intent.

Examples of Exact Quote vs. Intent Choices

Exact quote choices	Intent choices
Ex: "___, if you don't start processing more claims, we will have to let you go."	Ex: Explain to him that he needs to start producing or he will be fired.
Are more natural and hence maintain the realism	Are less natural and may detract a little from the realism
People can get hung up on the actual wording instead of the important content.	While people are less likely get hung up on the wording, they are more likely to not be as highly engaged.
Takes more effort *and* storytelling writing talent to write good exact quotes.	Easier to write for novices.

Guideline 35: Avoid numbering or lettering your choices whenever possible. In the real world you rarely if ever see your choices presented this way. Do everything you can to stay within the context of the scenario.

Interaction Component 4: Rich Feedback

Good feedback consists of both observable and hidden real-world (intrinsic) feedback, instructional (extrinsic) feedback, and scoring. (Note, while intrinsic and extrinsic are probably more correct, they are less well known. I use the terms real-world and instructional as I believe they are easier to understand and will communicate my intent better.)

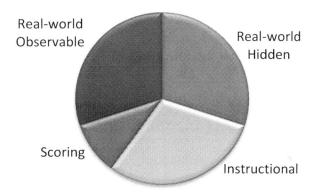

The learner absorbs content by reading about it and then by using it in activities. Providing feedback lets the learner know to what extent they have mastered the material and possibly reinforces the rationale for the correct path (the content). It lets them know if they have any misconceptions about the material.

Key Point 9: Rich feedback is key to learning from mistakes.

It has many functions, the main ones being:

- Supplying corrective information (the one we most think of)
- Identifying misconceptions or areas of misunderstanding
- Providing knowledge of impact of the choice made
- Dealing with motivation

> "When answers are wrong, people [e-learning authors] often simply point to the right answer and say, "This is the right one and this is why it is right!". People should be told **why** the wrong answer is wrong," Cliff Perry, personal email, 2013.

Warning 13: Avoid "Correct" "Incorrect" feedback. This takes the learner completely out of the scenario and back into the classroom. Focus instead on giving real-world feedback. Give likely impact, results, outcomes, consequences, etc. (See the next section for why.)

What Is Real-world Feedback?

Real-world feedback gives the likely *outcomes* or *results* of the choices. It enables learners to judge correctness for themselves. According to Allen (2007), intrinsic feedback is meaningful, memorable, and motivational.

We can use any of the following terms to talk about real-world feedback, which tie back to the situation about which the question was asked. Usually these are *observable* outcomes of the actions taken but not necessarily. Sometimes they are hidden.

Observable Outcomes	• Immediate reactions of people or systems
	• Immediate responses
	• Results
Hidden Outcomes	• Long-term effects, consequences, impacts
	• What people are thinking or feeling
	• Side-effects (the wrong drug causes liver damage)

"Impact" is especially important in writing real-world feedback. Sometimes we only think about the immediate results or consequences when there is really more to it if we consider it from a systems perspective or a longer time frame.

Examples of "Result" vs. "Impact" Feedback

The learner…	Result	Impact
1. Selects the wrong sales question to ask.	Got unexpected answer	Did not learn the true need, lost trust
2. Enters an order in wrong category	Order shipped but customer did not get proper discounts	Dissatisfied customer, possibly lost future business
3. Misses identifying a hazard	Tool fell and broke	Cost company money, black mark on record
4. Asks a motivated employee to do better without setting proper goals	Production dropped	Team did not win contest

Real-world feedback can incorporate any of the following:

- ✓ Observable outcomes such as change in employee behavior, customer reaction, effects on a system, etc.
- ✓ Reactions of a co-worker, boss, or other person (observable or not)
- ✓ Hidden outcomes - delayed changes
- ✓ Some measure of progress toward the goal if at all possible
- ✓ Graphic indicators when they are either part of the natural setting or they provide an indicator of things we would naturally sense like customer interest, boss's aggravation, pain level, phones sold, etc.

Further, in the real world results vary with the choice a person makes! Take the extra time it takes to give different feedback for each answer choice.

Guideline 36: Lest you forget, try to focus on the specific consequences of each choice. Provide a way for learners to access more information like a "Why" button. This allows you to expand on the course content.

Delayed Feedback

In some cases, to make it real-world, feedback should not be given immediately. You may want to consider a small amount of branching in your scenario where after the learner decides on an action choice, the path alters slightly.

> Ex: Learners select to give the patient aspirin for the headache which goes away now but returns later because the real cause was not addressed.

> Ex: Giving inappropriate discipline stops the fighting now but lower production later.

Instructional Feedback – Relevant Content

This is the easy part. Most of you are familiar with this already. You simply review the important content that is relevant to making a good decision.

Warning 14: Don't make your feedback too long or learners will not read it. You can introduce additional information if you want but be careful it is not too much.

Warning 15: Don't simply reference some earlier part of the course because learners are unlikely to take the time to go back and read it. Would you?

Examples

> Ex: Example 1: A video clip plays first and the learner is presented with: "As her coach, what do you recommend as the first thing that she should do with the products?"

Answer Choice Examples

Answer Choice	Real-world + Instructional Feedback
Wait for the next product course.	*Real-world part:* She finds out that the next course is not for several weeks. This will delay her selling anything in the meantime. *Instructional part*: Remember the guideline is that she should contact here manager when she is in doubt.
Start selling the products right away.	*Real-world part:* As she approaches several people to tell them about the product and finds out quickly that they ask questions she is not prepared to answer. *Instructional part:* She needs to have some product knowledge before attempting to sell to customers.
Read the product labels to learn more about them.	*Real-world part:* While this takes time, she learns some surprising things about the products and is now better prepared to sell them. *Instructional part:* This has proven to be the best approach to getting started.
Call the VP of Sales at headquarters and ask her.	*Real-world part:* Her line manager calls her up a bit later in the day and asks why she went over his head. She got him in trouble for appearing not to do his job. *Instructional part:* She should always contact her immediate manager first.

Ex: Example 2: "The customer has just asked about the requirements for using the product. How would you answer the customer's question?"

Answer Choice Examples

Answer Choice	Feedback
"To use ___, you must have a GPS capable device.	*Real-world part:* The customer frowns and does not say anything.
	Instructional part: Always explain special terms and acronyms to customers. Don't let them guess.
"When you purchase your new GPS capable devices, we would need to change your ___ to one that is needed for GPS."	*Real-world part:* The customer looks a little confused and asks another question.
	Instructional part: Always explain special terms and acronyms to customers. Don't let them guess.
"To use a Global Positioning System or GPS, all you have to do is be in a coverage area. The GPS icon will appear on the screen and 'GPS Ready'."	*Real-world part:* The customer looks satisfied with the answer and gives you a chance to explain further.

Tip 19: Alternative: You could ask learners, "What principle/fact should you have applied here? For a hint, click here." While that may be useful, note that it does take them out of the scenario.

Scoring

Detail the scoring for the interaction. If you are going to give overall results at the end of the scenario, now is when you make note of how they scored.

Other Kinds of Feedback

You can use some of these with individual questions while others are better suited for a set of questions. You can:

- Use dials, gauges, or progress bars to show increase in sales or productivity. They should look as much like the ones the company uses if possible.

- Use dials, gauges, or progress bars to show things we would naturally sense like customer interest or boss's aggravation, pain level, machine speed, phones sold, etc.
- Show an alternate image of the customer frowning.
- Show a picture of an accident.

Feedback Ideas from Ruth Clark

Ruth Clark (2013, p. 110) gave some examples of different kinds of feedback. Here is an abridged and augmented version of her table.

More Feedback Ideas

Domain	Observable Feedback	Hidden Feedback	Instructional Feedback
1. Interpersonal	Body language, questions, statements of other party; subsequent immediate actions (purchase, performance)	Attitude meter,	Guidelines or principles to use
2. Compliance	Consequences of policy violation	Delayed costs such as fines	How choices reflect policies, procedures, legal directives, etc.
3. Diagnosis, Assessment, Analysis, Evaluation	How patient, client, or equipment responds	Test or time cost, client satisfaction, long-term impact	Appropriateness of tests, accuracy of diagnosis tied to principles or guidelines

Try These Steps

Technique 15: How to write effective feedback for scenario interactions:

1. Visualize the situation described in the question.
2. Think about an answer choice and jot down:
   - What would be the short-term visible and hidden effects/results/consequences? I.e. what would you see change right away?
   - What could be possible long-term visible and hidden effects?
   - What questions could you ask in the feedback that would help them recall the relevant content?
   - What content do you need to list again to review?
3. Finally, think about how you will display this feedback:
   - Text
   - Photos of different expressions, other results (picture is worth a 1000 words but be sure to label it)
   - Gauges, meters, graphs, etc.
   - Audio, video, animation

Final Miscellaneous Guidelines for Feedback

Best Practice 23: Focus the feedback on the problem/task/job rather than on the learner. Avoid phrases like, "Good job." (Clark, Scenario-based e-Learning, 2013, page 108.)

Best Practice 24: Refine the question, choices, and feedback. It is not a simple path – write questions → write feedback. Most people cycle back and forth between the two.

As you write the feedback, you end up seeing the need to revise the choices. As you revise one choice, it affects another which in turn changes its feedback or even how the question is worded.

Best Practice 25: Using real-world feedback in combination with allowing the learner to try again, encourages experimentation.

Many learners will try several answer choices just to find out what the impact was, thereby learning even more from the exercise.

Interaction Component 5: The Support Available

In many cases, you will want the learner to access some reference material to properly answer the question. What information about the scene is immediately available and what is available for the asking? What are you going to make available to learners to help them answer the question? This is frequently referred to as resources and sometimes as scaffolding (because it supports the learning). Here is the list we covered earlier:

- (Library, Documentation, Policies and Procedures, xxx User Guide, ... Manager's Handbook, ...
- Description of the sales process – best put in the form of a real job aid
- Description of principles involved– best put in the form of a real job aid
- Analysis tools like calculators, spreadsheets
- Charts, graphs, diagrams– best put in the form of a real job aid
- Forms
- Glossary – maybe you can turn this into a dictionary or words from an expert
- Job aids
- Tips – possible position as memos or emails
- Questions to ask – possible position as memos or emails
- Briefings (1-2 pages of info) – possible position as memos or emails
- Examples

Best Practice 26: Allow the learner to ask questions to get more information on the current situation. I.e. do not describe everything. This makes things more realistic.

In real world you usually do not know all you need to know at first. You can get and do need a bit more information to make a good decision (improve judgment).

Gee's "just in time" and "on demand" approach is useful.

- "just in time" (when they can put it to use)
- "on demand" (when they want it)

Use the obstacles in the scenario scenes ("times") that "demand" that the learner know certain information. This sets up the "just in time" "on demand" condition which will enhance engagement, memory, and transfer back to the job.

Decide *what* you are going to make available, *when*, and *how*.

Support Considerations

1. What	•	Reference documents including handbooks, guides, policy manuals, management manuals, memory joggers, job aids, pocket guides, websites, etc.
	•	Simple tips, reminders, hints, advice
2. When	•	Always available like a menu that is in every page
	•	Clicking on work-related icons like books, manuals, file drawers, which allow the learner to access the content information
	•	Clicking on characters to obtain additional information about them
	•	When feedback is delivered for an interaction
3. How	•	Mousing over or clicking on buttons, checkboxes, hotspots, or menus
	•	Dragging objects to a location
	•	Touching locations on the screen

Interaction Component 6: Next Steps

If you need to, note how the learner's choice affects the remainder of the scenario.

- If you are branching, where does it go now?
- Are there delayed consequences of this choice?

Design Multiple Levels If You Have Time

Experienced employees will want more of a challenge than people who are new to the position. At the same time, you do not want to overwhelm the new employee with too much information. Because not all learners approach the scenario with the same level of experience, you may want to design multiple levels into your scenario and allow the learner to select the level at the beginning.

Tip 20: For critical skills, it is advisable to design multiple scenarios so that learners can get additional practice. Start with the one you just developed and change things.

Tip 21: For new learners, offer a tips button or maybe something like, "Can't decide? Click here to get a tip from the top sales person last year."

Technique 16: How to design multiple levels of difficulty:

1. Include hints for the easier levels.
2. Write easy and harder versions of the same question, one has more information or help buttons than the other.
3. Include harder questions in the more difficult versions.
4. Add time limits to make it more challenging.
5. Allow retries on the easier versions.
6. Allow moving back by showing the Back button or not
7. Incorporate debriefing after as part of the feedback of each question. "The customer just left the store. (natural internal feedback) Why do you think that happened?"

Step 6: **Finalize the Results, Results Section**

One of Gagné's nine events of instruction is assessing performance. The results section does this. Take whatever you are using for scoring that you selected back in your Rough Draft (pg. 82) and give them feedback on their overall performance.

Warning 16: Don't take the easy way out at the end. Don't just give a score and say "Congratulations. You passed. (Sorry you failed.)" If this is all you do, you lose some of the real power of a scenario.

Best Practice 27: When you present the results, connect their performance to how well they are mastering the material and likely future job performance.

Technique 17: How to write powerful Results page(s):

1. Give their overall performance indication, rating, or score.
2. Connect that with potential job performance.
3. Give an analysis so they can see *where* they need to improve.
4. When possible, do some debriefing.
5. Provide recommendations as to what to do next, especially for inadequate performance.

Give Feedback on Their Overall Performance

Whenever possible, couch their overall performance in job terms.

Ex: "Congratulations. You sold 6 cell phones today."

Ex: "It took you 2 hours to deliver that pizza. You probably would not get much of a tip."

Ex: "Your team's performance is up by 25%. Looks like you have mastered the teamwork principles and can lead a team."

Ex: "Your team went 45 days without an accident."

Ex: "You increased productivity/sales by ___. Looks like you are ready to move on to ___."

Ex: "You increased productivity/sales by only ___.

Ex: "Based on your score, it looks like you could do a great job coaching/leading your team."

Ex: "Based on your score, it looks like you could have problems coaching/leading your team."

Ex: "Based on your score, it looks like you could work safely in the plant."

Ex: "Based on your score, it looks like you could have problems working safely. Here's why. (Followed by analysis of specific areas where they did not do well)."

If you can, go a little deeper like some of these.

Ex: "Based on your score, it looks like you have a great knowledge of the product and could successfully explain it to a customer."

Ex: "Based on your score, it looks like your product knowledge is a little low. You will likely miss some sales."

Ex: "Well it looks like you know what is and what is not considered sexual harassment."

Ex: "Well it looks like you have a fair chance of making a serious mistake in the sexual harassment area."

Ex: "Your score indicates that you have several gaps in your understanding of the ___ procedure. This could cause some serious problems filing a claim.

If Possible, Give an Analysis

Best Practice 28: Help learners dig deeper into how they did and where they need to improve. Analyze their results and tell them which areas they need to spend more time on.

Your questions should tie to objectives and each of those objectives should have content to support it so it should not be too hard to track back and give learners an idea what they need to study more.

Ex: "Let's look at why."

Ex: "Let's take a closer look and find out where you did well and where you could improve."

Ex: You did well on ___ but not so well on ___."

Ex: "Your team increased production but your accident/waste went above company standards."

If possible, tie low scoring areas back to the job.

Ex: "You rated these rooms too low which means you are being too easy. Guests are likely to get the impression this is a cheap hotel."

Ex: "You missed quite a few safety violations. There is a good chance we could have an accident and cost the plant some serious downtime."

Ex: "You could do a better job explaining the new cell phone to customers. If you performed this way with real customers, you sales might be way down."

Ex: "You need to work more on applying coaching principles two and three. Coaching your way could result in low production and employee problems down the road."

Tip 22: When possible, give specific impact of low scores in a particular area.

Ex: "While you did well in water safety, it looks like you should brush up on fire safety to reduce the risk of fire hazards."

Ex: "You regularly rated the deficiencies too low which could result in a shoddy run-down appearance."

Ex: "You regularly rated the deficiencies too high which could result in spending money on low-priority items."

Ex: "Low attention to getting employees to take ownership of things can easily lead to reduced quality and low performance."

Debriefing

As I said earlier, **debriefing helps the learner remember the content longer, know where to spend more time, and see cause and effect better.**

Framing the Session

You have a couple of options – ideas to draw from should you decide you want to develop debriefing. You can drive it totally as *external* feedback or as *internal* feedback.

Instructional (External) Perspective

- Here is where you made a mistake.
- Here is how bad the mistake is.
- Here is how to avoid making the mistake in the future.
- This is how to remember not to make this mistake.
- This is what an expert would do.
- This is how an expert would know what to do.

- Here is what a co-worker would do.

Tip 23: But, telling someone where they need to improve is not quite as good as having them figure it out for themselves. It is okay and does help. The drawback is that is a bit like a lecture. Now I don't know about you, but I just *love to be lectured to.* ☺

Real-world (Intrinsic) Perspective

Your alternative is to reframe it as internal feedback that is *still* part of the scenario like this:

"Your manager calls you into his office first thing on the following Monday morning to go over the week and your decisions. He asks:

- Where do you think you made mistakes?
- For each mistake:
    - How bad do you think it was?
    - How can you avoid making it in the future?
    - How can you remember not to make it?
    - What do you think an expert would have done?
    - What do you think a co-worker would have done?
    - Why do you think the customer did not buy? (getting the learner to think about cause and effect)
    - What areas do you need to study more?"

It will take you more time to construct debriefing questions and answers but they would make good learning points. Here are a few examples.

- "How could you avoid making the mistake in the future?" Among the choices you provide would be to refer to the Memory Jogger.
- "What do you think an expert would have done?" Among the choices would be the content answer you are trying to get across. Your feedback to this question would be the content answer.

Provide Recommendations

Once you have finished with all the results and debriefing, give some recommendations as to what to do next.

Ex: "Looks like you need to review the ___ material in this course."

Ex: We recommend that you review the ___ section in this course and try again."

Ex: Save yourself some grief. Review the material in this course and try again."

Step 7: **Write the Wrap-up Section**

In this section, your job is to bring the whole course together, and, as it says, wrap things up. You can include:

- A summary of important points in *job-aid fashion*, not just listing the topics covered
- Next steps for the learner if you have not already done so in the Results section. What is the learner to do now? Take the next course? Report to the boss? Hold a practice session? Have a party?
- Congratulations
- A certificate

For more in-depth details on this section, see *Designing Effective e-Learning*.

Step 8: **Write the Support Section**

At this point in the storyboard, all you should have to do is go back over the interactions and create the support you listed as you wrote them.

- Additional on-demand content delivered at critical points during the execution of the scenario
- Reference documents (handbooks, guides, policy manuals, etc.)
- About this course, Help, References, etc. pages
- Intra/internet links
- Contact information – whom they can contact for additional information or with questions

Step 9: **Finish Up**

Well, you are almost done. Just a few things to wrap up before moving on to development in an authoring tool.

- Maximize realism.
- Check it over for common mistakes.
- Create an assets list so you can estimate the remaining effort.
- Review with stakeholders.

Maximize Realism

Hopefully you have been doing this along the way but you might have missed some opportunities. Go back over your whole course and especially the scenario and see where you can add realism or avoid detracting from it.

Technique 18: How to maximize realism:

When and where you can ...

1. Spend extra time completely describing the setting and characters.
2. Present the learner with a clear challenge at the beginning of the scenario.
3. Use the learner's name in a natural way like someone would on the job. Use their first name when possible if that is common. In some environments, like the military, they tend to use the last name rather than the first. Make it as real as possible.
4. Use pictures of real work environments.
5. Name your navigation buttons "See what happened" or "Move to the next room"
6. Present supporting content like it would be presented on the job like reference manuals, policy guides, etc.

Avoid:

× Simple recall questions.

- ✗ Check Answer or Submit buttons. Maybe give feedback when they move on to the next question.
- ✗ Back buttons in the scenario – rarely can you go back and revisit things. We do not have a time machine in reality so don't give your scenario one. They can do the whole thing over.
- ✗ Page numbers. Use a clock, calendar, miles, or other natural indication of progress.
- ✗ Counting things like points. Use natural metrics like dollars, production units, or accidents.

Make Sure You Avoided These Common Mistakes

Mistake	Description
1. Delivering too much	You have limited time. Don't try to crowd everything in. Do just the essentials.
2. Poor feedback	Avoid feedback that says "Correct" or "Incorrect." Use real-world feedback as well as instructional feedback.
3. Failing to use the word "you."	Design your scenario so that it connects with the learner. Use first and second person pronouns.
4. Using feedback to complement the learner	Avoid phrases that complement the ego like "Great work!" Focus instead on the impact of the decision and why it could have been better based on the content (Clark, 2013, p. 108).
5. Thinking you can design this in one pass	You will find that as you flesh-out one area it calls for changes in another. Be prepared to go back and make revisions. They will be fewer if you follow the tasks and steps in this book and get your reviews, but you will still have changes.

Mistake	Description
6. Failing to get learners to take ownership	What you want is for learners to take responsibility for their actions during the scenario. Ownership gives the scenario its power. • Avoid random numbers to determine consequences. • Avoid specifying the attitudes or values they should reflect in their role. Ex. avoid "You are a liberal … who supports …"

Estimate Remaining Effort

Before you go too much further, estimate the development effort. In addition to simple text and graphics, many courses call for additional assets such as:

- Audio clips
- Video
- Special graphics
- Animations
- Special photographs which may require an special shooting session
- Record steps in a computer procedure (Captivate®, Camtasia®)

These can require extensive effort to script and then produce. Create more than just an asset list. Get some idea of the effort and how long it will take. Some things can be done in four hours but it may take several weeks to get things scheduled.

Technique 19: How to estimate the remaining effort:

1. Create an asset list (see following table).
2. Estimate the effort to write the script or write out a detailed description of what is to happen.
3. Estimate the effort to actually create the asset – how many hours will it take to record that audio clip, create that animation, and take the photos.
4. Estimate the *elapsed* time it will take. Some tasks may only take an hour but trying to get that hour may be a bear. You have to work the task into other people's schedule or around all the other interruptions you have to your own schedule.
5. Itemize any special needs like release forms, getting on the CEO's calendar, scheduling with the plant, plant manager authorization, special recording equipment, acting talent, production experts (video editors, animators, etc.), legal requirements and approvals, and on and on. You know the drill.

Use something like the following table to estimate production effort, cost, and time-line.

Production Effort Estimation Form

Asset	Write Script/Descr Effort (Hrs.)	Production Effort (Hrs.)	Elapsed Time (Days)	Special Needs*
1. Build in authoring tool		20	5	
2. 4 audio clips	4	1	2	Sound studio
3. Opening video from CEO	1	1	14	CEO Video camera Video editor

Asset	Write Script/Descr Effort (Hrs.)	Production Effort (Hrs.)	Elapsed Time (Days)	Special Needs*
4. Production line photos	4	4	28	Plant authorization, high-res camera, photographer
5. Boiler animation	1	8	2	Animator

* Release forms, getting on the CEO's calendar, scheduling with the plant, plant manager authorization, special recording equipment, acting talent, and production experts (video editors, animators, etc.)

Review with Stakeholders and Update

Now that you have the final storyboard and a fair guess as to what is ahead, get it reviewed by stakeholders and other applicable specialists. Also, run the projected effort, cost, and timeline by your boss and the sponsor.

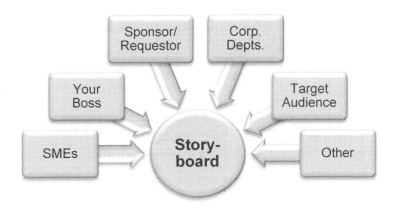

Stakeholders Who Need to Approve the Storyboard

Technique 20: How to assure support for development:

1. When you ask for stakeholders' review, make it clear *what* you want them to focus on in their review as shown below:

- SMEs—ask them to make sure the content is accurate and complete; in practice exercises and assessment questions, make sure that the answers flagged as the correct answers are in fact the correct ones and that the feedback is appropriate.
- The course sponsor(s) (to get buy-in)—ask for their overall impression, issues.
- Corporate departments—ask to be sure it complies with corporate guidelines.
- Members of the target audience—ask for their overall impression and if practice exercises and assessment questions clear.
- Another instructional designer—ask if it follows good instructional design practices. (www.eProficiency.com provides these services.)
- Someone who has language talents (an English major for example)—have them review it for word choice, grammar, etc. (Do this one last after all the other corrections have been entered.)

2. Tell them how to indicate changes.
   - Tell them to make corrections directly in the text in a different color (use the line through style to indicate text to delete i.e. abc).
   - Tell them they can enter feedback directly in the course in a different color or in the margins.
   - Have them add the date and initials to the storyboard file name (yyyy-mm-dd initials).
   - If you have more than one iteration of reviews, add a version number (v1) after the file name before sending it out.

3. When you send your reviewers the storyboard, be sure to get their agreement about *when* their review will be completed and have the feedback back to you so you can stay on schedule.

Critical Success Factors for "eLearning by Doing"

To ensure a solid effective course,

monitor these factors.

Factor	What You Need to Do
1. Focus	✓ If it doesn't contribute directly to the course purpose, get rid of it. Stay focused!
2. Nature of content delivery	✓ **Deliver the content in the context of the scenario**, a briefing for example.
3. Number of authors	✓ **For best results, get help writing the scenario description and interactions.** Focus on realism and challenge.
4. Interaction realism	✓ Present learners with realistic job-related settings. ✓ Place them in the situation. Make them an actor. ✓ Have them do realistic thought-provoking things such as give explanations to someone, make predictions, decisions, ask for information, make calculations, rate, or code items. ✓ Give them realistic answer choices. ✓ Give them rich real-world feedback and avoid "correct" and "incorrect."
5. Meaningful results	✓ **Give overall job-related results at the conclusion of the scenario.**

6.	Effective review	✓ Be specific as to what, how, and when you want feedback from your reviewers.
		✓ Have a fair estimate of what is left to do and get it approved by the key stakeholders.

Ben Pitman, the author, is available for consulting on e-learning design or development in Lectora. Here is his contact information:

Ben.pitman@eProficiency.com

678-571-4179 in Atlanta, GA

www.eProficiency.com to learn more

Appendix 1: "Forms" to Help with Design

Here you will find some forms I have used over the years. These are just some *ideas* for forms you could create to help you. Seems that no matter which one I use, it changes with the next project so I am reluctant to say "Here are the exact forms. Just print and you are done." These are more intended to be memory joggers and organizers to help you along the way. I recommend

- Rough Draft Form
- Storyline Form
- Interaction Form

Scenario Course Rough Draft Form

This can be done using a form like the one below or simply a list of section headings in something like MS Word®.

Section	Contents/Components
1. Opening Pages	Note anything special about these pages. Note negative case study if you have one.
2. Content	Describe the content in a few sentences and note where the content will come from.
3. Scenario Opening	Briefly describe the scenario challenge, interface/navigation instructions page(s), learner customization page(s) if any
4. Scenario Interaction Segments	Generally describe a few sample interactions and the kind of feedback you would get.
5. Scenario Results	Summary of how they did and Debriefing
6. Wrap-up	Summary of what was covered, key points to remember and next steps
7. Support	Popup pages containing any kind of support material used by learners

Or just:

Opening Pages
Content
Scenario Opening
Scenario Interaction Segments
Scenario Results
Wrap-up
Support

Storyline Form

This form is designed to be used while outlining the scenario and then *later* expanded when converting to a scenario. You may want to do this form in landscape mode so you have more room for the columns.

Who (all characters):

When (Environment):

Where (Environment):

Overall Scenario Goal:

Story and Obstacles

Situation: Who, what, where, when	Obstacle	Possible Questions for Interactions	Notes: Audio, animation, video, graphics

Interaction Form

Use one of these for each interaction. You can use the form table or simply use headings in a document.

Interaction (Scene) Components Form

Component	Description			
1. Description	Who, where, when, what's happening (surroundings, environment, setting, context)			
2. Decision (Question)	Write the question, usually in the second person. "What would you do?" "What would you tell the customer? Your boss?" "What is likely to happen next?"			
3. Choices	4. Rich Feedback			
	Observable Outcomes	Hidden/delayed Outcomes	Relevant Content	Scoring
A. ...				
B. ...				
C. ...				
...				
5. Support Available	Manuals, guides, etc.			
6. Next Scene				

1. Description

Who, where, when, what's happening (surroundings, environment, setting, context)

2. Decision (Question)

The question, usually in the second person, couched in job scene.

- Action: "What would you do/say?" "What would you tell the customer? Your boss?"
- Get information[1]: "What would you ask the customer?" "What diagnostic would you run?"
- Prediction[2]: "What would you tell your boss to explain why this happened?"
- Explanation[2]: "What would you say to the customer as to why this happens?"
- Calculate or code: "What is the new due date?"

3. Choices and Feed Back

While this part could be done without using a Word® table, Choices and Feedback sections work better if they are side by side – it is easier to ensure you have the right kind of feedback and that it all works together. I recommend that you do this one in landscape mode. I did it here in portrait mode to fit in the book.

	Observable Outcomes[1]	Hidden/delayed Outcomes	Relevant Content	Scoring
A. …				
B. …				
C. …				
…				

[1] Information from customer in response to the query, results of diagnostic, etc.

[2] Remember to keep these questions within the scenario context. Avoid simply saying, "What is likely to happen next?" or "What caused this?"

5. Support Available

- (Library, Documentation, Policies and Procedures, xxx User Guide, ... Manager's Handbook, ...
- Description of the sales process – best put in the form of a real job aid
- Description of principles involved– best put in the form of a real job aid
- Analysis tools like calculators, spreadsheets
- Charts, graphs, diagrams– best put in the form of a real job aid
- Forms
- Glossary – maybe you can turn this into a dictionary or words from an expert
- Job aids
- Tips – possible position as memos or emails
- Questions to ask – possible position as memos or emails
- Briefings (1-2 pages of info) – possible position as memos or emails
- Examples

6. Next Scene

If this applies, what happens next.

Appendix 2: Book Highlights

This is a quick review of the techniques, best practices, guidelines, key points, and warnings in this book. You can use it:

- To review the content and if you have questions, just go to that page and start reading.
- To look for something you read. Often I have gone back into a book looking for something and had to scan the whole book. Here you can read over the whole book in 10-11 pages and hopefully find what you are looking for or at least something close to it.
- Use it in design sessions to make yourself look like a scenario guru.

Before First Chapter

Warning 1: This guide it is not for everyone. It is only for the serious designers.—i

Introduction—1

Warning 2: Don't try to read this guide all at once.—5

Warning 3: Many e-learning designers and developers fruitlessly try to make their courses better by adding slick graphics, animations, audio, video, having a lot of things the learner to click on, and simple recall questions.—6

Technique 1: How to convince your boss or client to use a scenario:—19

Task 1: Define the Basis for Your Course—23

Step 1: Find Out Who Cares About This Training—24

Key Point 1: "People support what they create."—24

Technique 2: How to avoid unnecessary changes:—24

Step 2: Find Out What the Course Sponsor is Trying to Accomplish—26

Key Point 2: If you are not very clear about where you want the training to go (its end result), then there is a really good chance that what you achieve will be not be what is needed.—27

Key Point 3: If you can't write a purpose that connects the course to a business benefit, question the real value of the course.—28

Technique 3: How to draft a powerful course purpose:—29

Best Practice 1: If what you are considering including in the content or doing is not directly contributing to the purpose of your course, get rid of it!—30

Step 3: Nail-down Who the Trainees Are—31

Step 4: Define Specifically What They Need To Be Able To Do—35

Best Practice 2: Use your course purpose to drive your objectives and persist to find the necessary content.—35

Guideline 1: For scenario-based training, write goals that involve the learner doing something job related.—36

Technique 4: How to write motivating learner-focused performance objectives:—37

Best Practice 3: *"Start with reality-based learning objectives. As you design your course, keep reminding yourself of those objectives. That way your WBT [course] will be reality-based as well"* (Stone & Koskinen, 2002, p. 66).—42

Best Practice 4: Write course level performance objectives and topic level performance level performance objectives.—42

Warning 4: Limit each topic (maybe lesson) to three to five objectives.—43

Step 5: Review with Key Stakeholders—44

Best Practice 5: At the end of each task, you should have your design reviewed by the people who care.—44

Task 2: Collect Your Content—47

Step 1: Collect Basic Content—48

Best Practice 6: Be sure you have collected data on misconceptions and mistakes to use later when creating obstacles, questions, and question choices.—49

Best Practice 7: Use your objectives as a guide to determine whether or not the information is really needed. Ask, "What is the minimum information the learners need to achieve the objective?" That is what you include in your course.—49

Step 2: Collect Content for the Scenario—52

Best Practice 8: Get those war stories – stories of how people overcame significant (job related) barriers.—53

Key Point 4: IMPORTANT – making your scenario realistic requires more stories from the SMEs – especially when creating interactions and feedback. Be sure to identify and capture any kind of cause and effect.—53

Technique 5: How to collect war story information:—54

Technique 6: How to collect information on mistakes for the scenario:—54

Guideline 2: While you are gathering the content, look for cause and effect relationships because the interactions in your scenario will be decisions made by the learners.—55

Guideline 3: The lesson here is that your interactions can go many ways. Be sure you get all the perspectives so you can write realistic ones.—55

Best Practice 9: Be sure to gather content about outcomes. This information will be key to creating real-world feedback and a meaningful scoring system.—56

Step 3: Organize & Chunk Content—56

Best Practice 10: Organize your material around job tasks or steps rather than around product features, theory, or models when possible (Clark, 2008b, p. 184). This makes for greater interest and transfer to the job.—56

Step 4: Review and Revise Course Purpose and Objectives—57

Step 5: Review with Major Stakeholders—58

Task 3: Create a Rough Draft—61

Step 1: Briefly Outline How You Are Going to Deliver Your Content—64

Warning 5: Don't deliver too much content before having the learner use it.—64

Best Practice 11: Limit the amount of content you deliver, especially with a scenario. You want the learner to get involved quickly with applying the content. You can add other "lessons learned" along the way.—65

Step 2: Draft a Great Scenario Opening—65

Technique 7: How to write a great scenario beginning:—66

Guideline 4: Take these aspects (situation, problem, impact, need) and draft the opening to your scenario. You can use:—67

Guideline 5: You know you are done with this when you have described the circumstances that will allow learners to see that the content is important and give them the opportunity to use the content.—68

Guideline 6: You need the "Impact" aspect to help create your storyline, a sense of urgency, and possibly help you word the results section of the scenario.—69

Step 3: Plan the Interactions—71

Key Point 5: *"The key to the design of process exercises for employees involved in problem solving is to collect realistic case studies of common malfunctions, customer questions, and so forth that can be converted into practice exercises. "*Clark, 2008b, p. 13.—72

Guideline 7: Start with your performance objectives. Using them as a guide, make a list of the kinds of decisions learners need to make. Without worrying too much about the interface, draft a list of the decisions the learner should make (questions the learner should be able to answer).—72

Warning 6: Limit the number of different types of questions you use. While it may be fun to use different types, each time learners encounter a different type, they have to think a little about what to do rather than stay in the scenario. If you use just one or two types, how to answer the question will fall into the background and they will be able to focus on the scenario.—76

Guideline 8: Give some examples of feedback for the typical interactions you created earlier. You will need these for your prototype and to give stakeholders an idea of what to expect.—76

Guideline 9: Specify how the feedback is to be displayed. Is it going to be a popup window, a change in character expression, dials or gauges changing, etc.—76

Guideline 10: Try to focus on the consequences of each choice.—76

Guideline 11: Provide a way for learners to access more information like a "Why" button. This allows you to expand on the course content.—76

Warning 7: If you decide to use some type of branching, be prepared for testing to take considerably more time.—78

Step 4: Draft Scoring, Results, and Debriefing Approach—82

Best Practice 12: Try to design a scoring system that gives more information than just passed or failed. Most learners will master some parts of the content but not others. A good scoring system tells the learner what areas they need to review.—82

Guideline 12: If there is natural scoring method or way of measuring performance in the nature of your scenario, use the performance objectives. Summarize how learners did for each objective.—83

Warning 8: Avoid using things like collecting tokens or earning points unless you do that in the workplace. Remember – Transfer to the job is key.—83

Best Practice 13: Design your scoring so that learners earn more for better answers because this reflects the fact that the real world is not black and white but rather shades of gray.—84

Step 5: Make Strategic Decisions Regarding Media—85

Step 6: Draft the Interface—85

Step 7: Review with Stakeholders—91

Task 4: Build a Prototype—93

Key Point 6: Remember you goal with a prototype is to make sure everything is going to work as planned and your stakeholders approve the design.—94

Step 1: Create the Screen Layout—95

Step 2: Create Typical Pages—99

Best Practice 14: Once you have your typical background and navigation, create typical pages for each scenario section to give your reviewers a good feel for what the course will look like.—99

Guideline 13: Creating sample interactions is *the* most important part of the prototype. Using the list of typical interactions you created in the previous task, create a working prototype of each type of interaction including feedback and scoring.—100

Best Practice 15: Make sure your prototype works under all conditions, not just the first time interactions are encountered.—101

Step 3: Review with Stakeholders—102

Task 5: Draft a Storyline If Needed—105

Step 1: Envision a "Story-*world*", Not a Story—107

Technique 8: How to come up with a story-world:—108

Step 2: Use the Tried and True Hollywood Formula—109

Step 3: Review/Refine the Scenario Situation and Goal—110

Step 4: Identify Obstacles/Problems for Interactions—111

Guideline 14: Come up with more interactions (questions) than you need because you will likely throw some out later.—111

Guideline 15: Put these between the situation described in the opening scene and the goal.—111

Guideline 16: Now review the obstacles to be sure that if the learner overcomes the obstacles, they will the learning content be covered and getting closer to the goal.—111

Step 5: Write Character Descriptions—111

Step 6: Write the Story—112

Technique 9: How to create a storyline using the Hollywood formula:—112

Step 7: Remove the Boring Bits → Make It Fun—113

Guideline 17: Focus on challenge while remembering that not everyone likes competition.—113

Step 8: Review with Stakeholders—114

Task 6: Write the Final Storyboard—117

Guideline 18: Be consistent about how the learner interacts with the scenario. The more variety, the more the learner focuses on the technology and *not* on the scenario or the content.—120

Step 1: Select Your Storyboarding Tool—121

Technique 10: Effective use of a storyboard:—121

Step 2: Write Your Course Opening Section—121

Guideline 19: Make your course fit the culture of the work environment and the topic. If it is a serious topic, have a serious looking welcome page; if it is a casual topic or a casual work environment, give your welcome page a casual look.—122

Guideline 20: Keep this page relatively clean and make it dramatic. Use a minimum of text and some powerful relevant graphics if you have the budget for them.—122

Key Point 7: The benefits page is key to motivating the learner. If the value of this course is not obvious, you should make a strong case for taking it. If you can't write a good benefits page, you may have a stupid course on your hands.—125

Best Practice 16: List as many personal benefits to the learner as possible.—125

Best Practice 17: Set the stage for the content and briefly introduce the scenario. If you can, make it tie in somehow with the negative case study given earlier.—126

Step 3: Write Your Content Section—127

Technique 11: How to write the content section – short version:—128

Guideline 21: Keep the tone and language in keeping with a briefing or within the context of the scenario for greatest effect.

Talk directly to the learner as though the boss was giving the briefing.—128

Step 4: Write Your Scenario Opening Pages—129

Technique 12: How to write effective opening pages for the scenario:—129

Best Practice 18: If you can, use their name on this page. If you do, use it like it would be used on the job. Sometimes this is the last name instead of the first.—130

Step 5: Write the Scenario Interactions—132

Best Practice 19: Make sure your interactions have the learner *apply* what they have learned.—132

Technique 13: How to write effective interactions for the scenario:—132

Best Practice 20: Before you get into writing the details of the interactions, finalize your scoring method. It can make a big difference in how you write your interactions.—133

Best Practice 21: Before you write all the details for each interaction, outline them all to make sure they flow well *and* that all your objectives are covered. Once you start writing the interaction, you can easily get lost in the details and forget some important questions to ask.—133

Technique 14: How to be sure all your performance objectives are covered:—134

Best Practice 22: Review our questions and objectives and ask yourself, "Will the questions for each objective ensure that the learner has achieved the objective?" (I.e. are these the right questions to be asking?)—134

Guideline 22: Allow for experimentation – allow the learner to try one solution and see what happens, learn from any mistakes, and then try again. No, not all learners will try again, but many will.—135

Guideline 23: Introduce additional content by providing things like icons they can click to get more information.—135

Guideline 24: Scenario and character development are far more important than graphics. If you have limited budget, put the energy into the scenario description and go lighter on the graphics.—135

Warning 9: Avoid recall questions as much as possible -- questions that cannot be put in context of the scenario.—140

Warning 10: Do not make the questions too easy or ridiculous because your scenario will become less interesting to the learner. Do you like playing a game where you know all the answers?—140

Guideline 25: Stop thinking of questions you are going to ask the learner and think about the decisions they will make on the job.—140

Warning 11: Avoid True/False questions as they are usually too simplistic for scenarios and rarely if ever does a work situation call for True or False decision as such.—142

Warning 12: Avoid matching except when labeling a diagram or something similar. If you are trying to sort things out, use a drag a drop. A bunch of crisscrossed lines is not memorable.—142

Key Point 8: Poor answer choices can ruin the best scenario question.—142

Guideline 26: Keep the choices within the context of the scenario, not external type questions – more or less real world decisions that will need to be made.—142

Guideline 27: Make their answers matter.—142

Guideline 28: The choices should use shades of gray if possible. The world is not black and white for the most part. Give answer choices that are distinct but different shades of gray.—143

Guideline 29: The choices should be a reasonable level of difficulty. Do not make them too hard because this will frustrate the learner.—143

Guideline 30: The choices should be straightforward. Avoid compound answer choices that use the word "and." Instead, break the answer choices apart and have the learner "Check all that apply."—143

Guideline 31: Present choices in a logical order. If the question has numeric choices, present them in numerical order (10, 20, 30, 40 not 20, 40, 30, 10).—143

Guideline 32: Make them similar length. People know that the longer answers are more likely to be correct.—143

Guideline 33: Make the answer choices parallel in construction (singular/plural, verb tense, a/an).—143

Guideline 34: Avoid "None of the above" or "All of the above". First of all, this is not very realistic and will draw learners out of the scenario. And, here are some more reasons.—144

Guideline 35: Avoid numbering or lettering your choices whenever possible. In the real world you rarely if ever see your choices presented this way. Do everything you can to stay within the context of the scenario.—145

Key Point 9: Rich feedback is key to learning from mistakes.—146

Warning 13: Avoid "Correct" "Incorrect" feedback. This takes the learner completely out of the scenario and back into the classroom. Focus instead on giving real-world feedback. Give likely impact, results, outcomes, consequences, etc. (See the next section for why.)—146

Guideline 36: Lest you forget, try to focus on the specific consequences of each choice. Provide a way for learners to access more information like a "Why" button. This allows you to expand on the course content.—148

Warning 14: Don't make your feedback too long or learners will not read it. You can introduce additional information if you want but be careful it is not too much.—148

Warning 15: Don't simply reference some earlier part of the course because learners are unlikely to take the time to go back and read it. Would you?—148

Technique 15: How to write effective feedback for scenario interactions:—152

Best Practice 23: Focus the feedback on the problem/task/job rather than on the learner. Avoid phrases like, "Good job." (Clark, Scenario-based e-Learning, 2013, page 108.)—152

Best Practice 24: Refine the question, choices, and feedback. It is not a simple path – write questions → write feedback. Most people cycle back and forth between the two.—152

Best Practice 25: Using real-world feedback in combination with allowing the learner to try again, encourages experimentation.—152

Best Practice 26: Allow the learner to ask questions to get more information on the current situation. I.e. do not describe everything. This makes things more realistic.—153

Technique 16: How to design multiple levels of difficulty:—155

Step 6: Finalize the Results, Results Section—155

Warning 16: Don't take the easy way out at the end. Don't just give a score and say "Congratulations. You passed. (Sorry you failed.)" If this is all you do, you lose some of the real power of a scenario.—155

Best Practice 27: When you present the results, connect their performance to how well they are mastering the material and likely future job performance.—156

Technique 17: How to write powerful Results page(s):—156

Best Practice 28: Help learners dig deeper into how they did and where they need to improve. Analyze their results and tell them which areas they need to spend more time on.—157

Step 7: Write the Wrap-up Section—160

Step 8: Write the Support Section—160

Step 9: Finish Up—161

Technique 18: How to maximize realism:—161

Technique 19: How to estimate the remaining effort:—164

Technique 20: How to assure support for development:—165

References

★ *indicates top choices*

Aldrich, C. (2004). *Simulations and the Future of Learning.* San Francisco, CA: Pfeiffer – This book is on simulations, not scenarios. While they are a lot more realistic, they take a lot more effort, talent, and technical resources to implement. However, many of the ideas and principles are applicable to scenarios.

Allen, M. (2003). *Michael Allen's Guide to e-Learning.* Hoboken, New Jersey: John Wiley & sons, Inc.

Allen, M. (2007). *Designing Successful E-learning.* San Francisco, CA: Pfeiffer

★ *Clark, Ruth (2013). Scenario-based e-Learning. San Francisco,* CA: John Wiley & Sons, Inc. – Probably the best book out there for research and how to apply it to e-learning.

Crawford, Chris (2005) *Chris Crawford on Interactive Storytelling.* Berkeley, DA: New Riders.

★ Gee, J.P. (2003). *What Video Games Have to Teach Us About Learning and Literacy.* New York: Palgrave Macmillan.

Gee, J. P. (2007). *Good Video Games and Good Learning: Collected Essays on Video Games, Learning and Literacy.* New York: Peter Lang.

Gibbons, A.S. & Fairweather, P.G. (1998). Computer-Based Instruction: Design and Development. Englewood Cliffs, NJ: Educational Technology Publications, Inc. (This is an excellent book but is quite heavy reading.)

Kathleen Iverson's article (Feb. 2008) on *Engaging the E-Learner: Interaction is Not Education. e-magazine.*

Kuhlmann, Tom (2008). *Rapid E-learning Blog.* http://www.articulate.com/rapid-elearning/heres-how-to-build-your-next-e-learning-scenario/

Kuhlmann, Tom (2008). *Rapid E-learning Blog.* http://www.articulate.com/rapid-elearning/heres-how-to-build-your-next-e-learning-scenario/

Mager, R. F. (1988). *Making Instruction Work.* Belmont, CA: David S. Lake Publishers. (Check book sellers for a current edition.) (This is a good book to get started on instructional design.)

Morrison, G.R., Ross, S.M., Kalman, K., & Kemp, J.E. (2011). *Designing Effective Instruction, Sixth Edition.* Hoboken, NJ: John Wiley & Sons. (Contains good coverage of how to do a needs analysis.)

Pitman, Benjamin (2013). *Designing Effective eLearning: A Step-by-Step Guide.* Suwanee, GA: eProficiency, Inc. Ben is available for consulting on e-learning design or development in Lectora. Here is his contact information:
- Ben.pitman@eProficiency.com
- 678-571-4179 in Atlanta, GA
- www.eProficiency.com to learn more

Prensky, M. (2007). *Digital Game-Based Learning.* St Paul, MN: Paragon House.

Quinn, Clark (2005). *Engaging Learning.* San Francisco, CA: Pfeiffer.

Stone, D.E. & Koskinen, C.L. (2002). *Planning and design for high-tech Web-based training.* Norwood, MA: Artech House.

Ward, D. & Elkins, D. (2009). *E-Learning Uncovered: From Concept to Execution.* Jacksonville, FL: Alcorn, Ward, & Partners.

Index

A
action decisions. *See* interactions: action decisions
activity. *See* interactions
All of the above, 144
Allen, M., 43, 131, 146
animation, 6, 72, 85, 100, 152, 163
audio, 8, 31, 33, 72, 85, 100, 124

B
Back button, 87, 97, 132, 155, 162
benefits, 28, 124, 125
branching. *See* interactions:branching
business case. *See* course purpose4

C
calculation decisions. *See* interactions: calculation decisions
case study, 12, 14, 119, 121
Case Study, 124, 126

Clark, R., 1, 6, 8, 10, 11, 12, 16, 52, 53, 56, 70, 72, 86, 151, 152, 162
coding decisions. *See* interactions: coding decisions
corporate department, 26, 166
course purpose, 3, 26, 27, 29, 36, 49, 57, 123
course sections, 62
    Content, 64, 127
    Course Opening, 121
    Scenario Interactions, 71, 132, *See also* interactions *for details*
    Scenario Opening, 65, 129
    Scenario Results, 82, 155
    Support, 160
    Wrap-up, 160
criteria, 43
Critical Success Factors, 45, 58, 92, 103, 114, 166

D
debriefing, 84, 86, 101, 155, 156, 158

diagnosis decisions. *See* interactions: diagnosis decisions

E
Elkins, D., 133
enabling objectives. *See* performance objecives
exercise. *See* interactions
expectations, 126, *See also* performance objectives
explanation decisions. *See* interactions: explanation decisions

F
feedback. *See* interactions:Feedback component, *See* interactions: feedback

G
games, 8, 14, 90, 97, 113
Gibbons, A.S., 37
goal. *See* course purpose *or* scenario goal
graphics, 6, 7, 9, 74, 94, 101, 109, 122, 135, 140, 163
guidance. *See* interactions:Support component

H
Help button, 97
Hollywood formula, 109

I
interactions, 71, 132
    action decisions, 73, 138
    behavior considerations, 87, 101
    branching, 70, 78
    calculation decisions, 73, 139
    Choices component, 142
    coding decisions, 74, 139
    computer question types, 74
    Decision (question) component, 137
    decision classes, 73, 137
    decisions, 72, 100
    Description component, 136
    diagnosis decisions, 73, 139
    explanation decisions, 73, 138
    feedback, 76, 88, 89, 145
    Feedback component, 145
    form, 135
    levels, 154
    Next Steps component, 154
    obstacles, 54
    prediction decisions, 73, 137
    scoring, 133, 155
    situation, 72
    Support component, 76, 86, 153
intrinsic feedback. *See* interactions:feedback

J
job analysis, 50

L
learner's name, 86, 161

M
Mager, R. F., 43
Morrison, G.R., 29
motivation, 33, 36, 65, 124, 130, 146
myths, 9

N
None of the above, 144

O
objectives. *See* performance objectives
obstacles, 49, 53, 54, 107, 108, 109, 110, 111, 112,

114, 154, *See also* storyline:obstacles
organization style
   basis for objectives, 38

P

performance objectives, 35, 37, 38, 45, 72, 83, 111, 134
Perry, C., 10, 11, 67, 129, 146
popup window, 71, 76, 88, 89
prediction decisions. *See* interactions: prediction decisions
prototype, 93
   screen layout, 95
   typical pages, 99

Q

questions. *See* interactions

R

realism, 161
real-world feedback. *See* interactions:feedback
remediation. *See* interactions: feedback
results, 82, 155

S

scaffolding. *See* interactions:Support component
scenario goal, 4, 82, 110
scoring, 82, 155
shades of gray, 56, 84, 143
situation descriptor, 72, 100

SME. *See* subject matter expert
sponsor, 43, 48, 166
stakeholders, 17, 21, 24, 44, 45, 48, 64, 71, 74, 76, 86, 93, 94, 95, 102, 103, 107, 114, 121, 161, 165, 168
Stolovitch, H.D., 31
Stone, D.E., 42
storyboard, 117
storyline, 105
   obstacles, 111
   story, 112
story-world, 107
student name. *See* learner's name
subject matter expert, 25, 50, 58, 97, 108, 114, 166
support. *See* interactions:Support component

T

target audience, 21, 25, 31, 32, 34, 44, 102, 166
task analysis, 50
terminal objective. *See* course purpose
tests, 17

V

video, 9, 31, 85, 100

W

war stories, 21, 22, 48, 53, 54, 55, 56, 59, 108, 112
Ward, D., 133

Manufactured by Amazon.ca
Bolton, ON